Love
Without The Drama™

Love
Without The Drama™

*Why Settle
When Relationships Can Sizzle?*

Lynetta Jordan

SpeakLife Publishing

Unless otherwise indicated, all Scripture quotations are based on the *King James Version* of the Bible.

Scripture passages or verses paraphrased by the author are based on the *King James Version* of the Bible or *The Amplified Bible*.

Scripture taken from THE AMPLIFIED BIBLE, Old Testament copyright © 1965, 1987 by the Zondervan Corporation. The Amplified New Testament copyright © 1958, 1987 by The Lockman Foundation. Used by permission.

Cover/Interior Images Developed from Microsoft Clip Art Media. ©2006 Microsoft Corporation. All rights reserved. Used by permission.

Love Without The Drama™

ISBN: 978-0-615-42533-7
Copyright © 2010 by Lynetta Jordan
All Rights Reserved.
Printed in the United States of America

SpeakLife Publishing House
"The Words I Speak They Are Spirit and Life." John 6:63
Mission: *Psalms 26:7*   Vision: *Psalms 68:11*

Speaklife Publishing
P.O. Box 1791
Elizabeth City, NC 27906

Library of Congress Cataloging-in-Publication Data: An application to register this book for cataloging has been submitted to the Library of Congress.

No parts of this book may be reproduced or transmitted in any form by any means, digital, electronic or mechanical--including photocopying, recording, or by any information storage and retrieval system--without written permission from the publisher.

The contents of this book are not to be considered as specific relationship advice. Any advice given is not guaranteed or warrantied by the author, and it may not be suitable for every factual situation. The author and publishing house assume no responsibility or liability for the relationship results of any of its audience.

———————————————————————

To: _____
From: _____
Date:_____

Your Relationship Destiny
Can Be So Much Better Than Your History!

God Wants You To Experience
Love Without The Drama!

By
Lynetta Jordan
"The Motivator"

———————————————————————

Dedication

My Entire Life
Is Dedicated To My Lord and Savior Jesus Christ!

My Journey Has Not Been Easy, But It Has Been Worth It.
Thank You For Healing Every Broken Place In My Heart
And For Being With Me All Of The Way, All Of My Life.
You Have Transformed My Trials Into Triumphs, Turned
My Tests Into Testimonies And My Misery Into Ministry.
I Am Honored To Be Gifted By You.
You Alone Are Worthy. There Is None Like You!

This Book Is Dedicated To
All The Virtuous Young Women God Has Blessed Me To
Mentor And Exemplify His Love, Life And Power!

And

The Loving Memories Of

My Unforgettable Mother
A Truly Phenomenal And Godly Woman
Who Was Happily Married To My Dad Close To 40 Years.
Together They Demonstrated Secure And Confident
Love Without The Drama

And

My Faith-Filled Grandparents
Who Were Closely Knitted Together For Over 65 Years And
Delighted In Each Other's Presence Even In Their Last Days.

Love Without The Drama™
Your Relationship Dreams Can Come True!

Contents

Preface
Introduction

ACT I
♥ Leaving Drama So You Can Live Your Dream ♥

1. Deliver Me From Drama!	13
2. Love Games	43
3. Heal Me From Heartbreak	59
Am I Bitter or Better?	

ACT II
♥ Defining The Dream ♥

4. Three Things Every Woman Wants	93
5. Three Things Every Man Needs	101
6. Marriage Truths, Myths and Mysteries	119
7. Wisdom for the Single and Seeking	141

ACT III
♥ Discovering Your Dream ♥

8. Love And Sports	169
Strategies For Relationship Success	
9. Security Matters	177
The Importance of Protecting Your Relationship	
10. Love Without The Drama	197
Why Settle When Relationships Can Sizzle?	

Preface

Hello. I'm Lynetta. It is an honor to *finally* meet you. Really, it is. You have no idea what experiences paved the roads I traveled to reach this destination and cross paths with yours.

Though our life stories are distinctly different, it interests me that you and I have one thing in common. Similarly, our relationships have not all been fairy tales. In fact, some of them have been two scenes short of a horror movie. Despite our scarred histories; however, we both unmistakably desire to improve our present and future relationships with the hope of experiencing maximized, more fulfilling lives. Our diverse paths have led us to the same heartfelt desire, to love and be loved--for real.

Countless people have lost faith in having a great relationship. Many battle-wounded men and women have bandaged bruises, but not been healed from bad breakups and failed marriages. As a result, plenty spiral downward into disastrous, dissatisfying rebound relationships when they do not apply spiritual antiseptic to heal their wounds.

You can experience healing and learn to love again even after multiple broken relationships. I composed this book to equip, encourage and empower you to experience relationships the way God originally intended them to be-- divinely orchestrated, mutually satisfying and personally fulfilling--when a destiny-connected man and woman complement *and* complete one another.

As we lay the foundation for our new friendship, I must be honest with you. I did not write this book alone. I have a silent partner who speaks ever so loudly. His name is Jesus. I typed each letter with the divine inspiration of God as Holy Spirit breathed life into every word, line, sentence, paragraph and page. He is the One who makes spiritual revelations applicable to everyday life.

Jeremiah 29:11 declares that God has plans to prosper and not harm you, to give you hope and an expected end. So as His ambassador, filled with His love and strength, I pour out of His heart into yours to restore you to health and launch you into the phenomenal future He desires for you. 3 John 2 says, "Beloved, I wish above all things that you would be in health and prosper, even as your soul prospers." The Lord clearly desires that your emotions, a component of your soul, be prosperous, too.

Like a virus, misery felt from unsuccessful intimate relationships has the potential to infect every area of your life. God is a healer, not just of physical ailments, but He has sent His word to heal our emotional issues, too.

Finally, I ask your forgiveness for delaying to write what God placed in my heart. After a period of procrastination, I was awakened when I realized God was counting on me as you were counting on Him for healing, understanding and empowerment. It is an honor to be chosen by God.

My own journey was not easy, but it was worth it. I now know that I went through love's valleys to help lead you out. My friend, prepare for a journey of joy and inspiration. God wants you to experience *Love Without the Drama*.

Introduction

Yes, You Can Journey From Relationship Drama To Your Relationship Dream *Without Going To Sleep!*

When you love better, you live better. That's what I believe. So tell me, is your relationship sizzling or fizzling? Whether you are single, happily married, married and miserable, distressed or divorced, God breathed life into this book for *you* to experience greater relationship success.

God still makes house calls. Consider this *your* time of refreshing--a private, relaxing counseling session full of godly wisdom, inspiration and emotional healing that has come to where you are. As you read on, honestly reflect on *your* personal life, not everyone else's. This is *your* time.

At the initiation of every good relationship, most friends have a discussion of "the rules"--what they like and don't like, what they must be open-minded about and what they cannot live without. As I unveil my heart to yours, let's remember the Golden Rule and three "rules of respect."

First, let's open our hearts and be truthful to ourselves. Second, let's be willing to consider new perspectives and fresh ideas that possess the power to deliver us from the bondage of a disastrous past. Third, though our genders, complexions, financial and marital statuses may vary, let's acknowledge that we all have the same longing--to be truly loved and celebrated by dates/mates of the opposite sex.

Finally, it is my desire for *Love Without The Drama* to inspire you so much that you discuss it in your bookclubs, recommend it to all of your social networks and purchase additional copies to bless coworkers, relatives and friends.

ACT I

Leaving Drama
So You Can Live
Your Dream

CHAPTER ONE
Deliver Me From Drama!

*Your relationship destiny does **not** have to repeat your history.*
- Lynetta Jordan

Love is a two-way street. That's what I said to myself as I calculated the costs of a dead end relationship that had drained and depleted my emotional account. He felt secure and was confident my care for him was genuine; however, he now treated me like reserve funds--not a priority for daily transactions, but there just in case he needed me.

He had misinterpreted my meekness as weakness. I wasn't married to him, but holding on to my initial hope of his potential to be my mate was not working either after a few years. He still chose to love the world more than God. As I compared my true self-worth to the obvious negative return on my heart's investment, I knew it was time for a change. If I wanted to experience a prosperous relationship again, I would have to withdraw any remaining funds and deposit my treasure elsewhere. I desired and deserved true friendship, spiritual fellowship and an abundance of fun and romance. Convinced I could have them all in one man, I would have to change banks and reinvest my first class love into an appreciating, not depreciating asset. I knew that I might have to wait for my God-ordained mate--a fun-loving, non-narcissistic Christ-like man who would abound in love for God and me--but experiencing the overflowing return in my life and ministry would be worth the wait!

It was time to be free from drama and finally experience the best in life and love that God had destined for me. I acknowledged my frailty--that I was not strong enough to disconnect from this man on my own--so the Lord severed every tie and empowered me to detach myself from his drama. With God's strength and power, I let go of the past so I could possess the promise of a bright future. My release of that unhealthy relationship opened the door for me to embrace a love-filled future. As I yielded my will to God's perfect will, I walked through that door one step at a time. Immediately, genuine love showed up in my life.

Like me, you can choose a better life. Love does not have to keep you in a downward spiral or going in circles. Neither do you have to repeat the mistakes of your family or friends. Instead of repeating that drama, you can choose to live drama free. You have the power to change your life!

You, my friend, may have experienced and endured some of life's drama-filled relationship storms, but I have breaking news! The forecast is now favorable for you! The sun is breaking through the dark, gloomy clouds of misery, dissatisfaction and depression that have lingered around you much too long. Clear blue skies and a colorful rainbow are scheduled to appear after your emotional storm concludes. Your future outlook is much brighter than your past. You, yes you, can have and enjoy a successful, drama-free relationship in the days and years ahead.

A Totally Fulfilling Relationship: God's Original Idea!

Whether you see the love glass as half full or half empty, you need to know that it is God's desire for you to experience abundant relationship success. Perhaps you feel like you have stumbled in the dark for years trying to get to the relationship of your dreams. Whether you are currently married, single or divorced, knowing that God truly cares about what matters to you can radically improve your life!

Contrary to the beliefs of many, making sure you attend church regularly is not God's only concern. He wants to be involved in every aspect of your everyday life. III John 2 says, "Beloved I wish above all things that you would be in health and prosper, even as your soul prospers." Your soul is where your emotions reside. Clearly, it is God's desire for you to be prosperous--to be overflowing and have more than enough spiritual and natural health, wealth and love.

Genesis, the very first book of the Bible, reveals the story of the creation of the first relationship. When God saw that all the living creatures had mates but Adam was alone, He decided in His infinite wisdom to create a helpmeet for him. In the second chapter of Genesis, God put Adam to sleep under holy anesthesia, touched his heart and removed his rib to create Eve, a suitable, comparable and complementary woman made especially for and from him.

When Adam, the first man, woke up from supernatural surgery, he was in awe of the natural beauty his eyes beheld. Adam was absolutely ecstatic! Eve was God's custom, tailor-made wife for him--a divine original, not a random selection. However, Eve's beauty was beyond her silky smooth skin. His fascination and magnetic attraction toward Eve surpassed her lips, hips, and fingertips.

To have lasting *love without the drama*, relationships require more than physical attraction. In today's world, people are often so enraptured with physical beauty that they don't delve deeper to discover a date's or mate's character. Online classifieds and newspaper personal ads highlight natural attributes--hair and eye color, weight, height and even the size of sexual organs. The significance of developing friendship through lengthy conversations and shared activities is often underestimated. While her coca-cola figure or his six pack abdomen may certainly capture one's eyes, it takes more than outward attributes to maintain your attraction to someone you will live with daily. Physiques may change, but enjoying your mate as your best friend will help keep you committed and in love.

Adam and Eve were also spiritually attracted. This divine couple had God's and each other's chemistry bubbling within them. Eve was so much like him that she could have been his spiritual twin. Adam was drawn to her because she was formed from his rib. When he laid eyes on her, Adam recognized his own reflection in his God-given companion. Eve was like a mirror to Adam's soul.

Adam was blessed with a divine mate to share the joy of God's creation. Reconnected with his missing piece, he was complete. Eve was made from him. God made them for each other. As Adam gazed on his God-ordained wife he shouted, "This is bone of my bone and flesh of my flesh!" Adam agreed with God that *everything* He made was good!

Identity Drama. *Don't trade your destiny for a temporary fix.*

Today's man still searches and longs for his missing rib--the drama-free woman who will complete, complement, and excite him! And today's woman still longs to be found by the drama-free man God created her specifically for. But sometimes people get in a hurry. When *you* rush to choose a date or mate before you are healed, you will have drama!

When you are hurting and not yet healed, it is not wise to speed into dating or marriage. When encountering the drama of overwhelming emotional pain, your self-perception and esteem may be temporarily altered. Subconsciously, the date or mate *you* choose will be your mirror--a vision of how you view yourself *at that present moment.* This is a dangerous place because in that condition, you will identify yourself in another hurting person. Though he or she reflects your temporary state, the danger is he or she does not possess your eternal purpose. As time progresses, you will feel the obvious misfit.

Think of a lock and key. Many keys may appear to be the "one" that will open a door. Some "almost" work--they slide into the groove, but do not turn. When you settle and do not wait for God's key (date or mate), you can't receive the blessings He has waiting for you behind love's door.

When God heals and restores your emotional health, it can be excruciatingly painful to find yourself miserable with and maybe even married to someone who does not hold your destiny or dreams. A man may realize that this woman, identified during his season of emotional pain, is NOT his true missing rib. That heartache is drama indeed.

Your ability to see clearly drastically decreases when you are rebounding from love lost. Without corrective lenses, you may think you are in love when you really are only infatuated. More disappointment and relationship drama can be avoided when you learn *not* to date or marry a person based on his or her *potential*, but the brutally honest truth and *reality* of who a person is *at that moment*.

It is dangerous, but not uncommon to have near-sighted or far-sighted love vision. But, it needs to be 20/20 before you dare drive forward into the future together. Too many couples enter the long-term marriage commitment without a thorough love vision check. Still others take their exams, but ignore the results and refuse to correct vision before it results in a substantial headache and heartache.

Act on your moment of truth. Some fiancés' hearts get them in trouble a second time when they do not back out of an engagement or marriage. They struggle with saying "no" and don't feel strong enough to handle what fickle people with their own love drama may think or say. Previously made verbal and financial obligations, twisted religious beliefs, pride, fear of embarrassment and future retaliation also keep them bound and moving forward with the wrong relationship. They may even wed secretly to avoid confrontations with the truth. No reason is worth you living miserably. It is respectable that you consider another's feelings, but you must first *love yourself enough* to act on the truth when he or she is not God's chosen mate. God will not be mad at you. He will help everyone heal and put you on the path of *the* mate He created just for you.

Unlike obtaining a driver's license, acquiring a marriage license does not require proof of corrected vision. When a person knows that a fiance' is not his or her God-ordained mate, he or she must make a serious choice--to act based on God's truth and wisdom, his or her fleshly pride or the fear of man's opinions. (Some Christians crumble to the fear of man.) When he or she is unwilling to humble him or herself and withdraw the engagement--what he or she may consider a hard thing to do--that decision automatically initiates a harder consequence, a miserable marriage. Refusing to take God's way of escape is like choosing an active prison sentence over probation or total freedom.

Revenge, animosity, legal sex alone, pleasing people and any other wrong marriage motive can lead you to sign up for longtime pain and bondage with divorce or death as the only escape. Most clear thinking people would rather be single and free than married and feel like they are behind bars. Is the seriousness of this drama coming clearer now?

People who override God's voice, fear man's voice and then bind themselves to misery later feel obligated to camouflage their marital dissatisfaction and dysfunction. Unhappy, they lie to themselves, pretend for others, suffer secretly and delay God's dream for them. Some convince themselves to cope by standing like an Army cadet on II Timothy 2:3, "Endure hardness as a good soldier of Jesus Christ," however; they misinterpret its context. Paul was admonishing Timothy to endure suffering encountered while walking in God's perfect will, *not* advising him to continue suffering from the error of choosing his own will.

That's pretty deep isn't it? But it's the truth. Suffering for righteousness sake and suffering for foolishness sake are distinctly different. If you haven't figured out the source of your suffering yet, examining your true feelings may help bring clarity and an answer to that big one word question--WHY?

Emotionally, how have you been feeling in the midst of your trial--joyful and somewhat honored to be going through it for God's sake or unhappy and mostly regretful? Though all trials have tough moments, your spirit feels an inner joy when you suffer as Paul did, because you are such a living example of Jesus Christ that you are counted worthy to suffer with and for Him. But you feel a miserable, lingering melancholy when you are suffering because of your own mistakes.

Which one describes how you have been feeling? If the answer surprises you, do not hesitate to pray and ask God to show you the error of your own way and help you to confess it. He made you and knows you, so you don't have to be embarrassed expressing your true feelings to Him. Cry if you need to, but most importantly, surrender your will to God's perfect will. Ask Him to help you get in line with His perfect will for your life so you can fully please Him. I'm sure He has been waiting for this moment of truth. God truly is able to bring your suffering to an end.

Now that you understand that point, let's take our discussion to another level. We must also be careful not to confuse suffering for "righteousness" sake with suffering for "rightness." There can be a thin line between the two.

"Rightness" is your overwhelming desire to be right or at least look like you are right (and religiously upright) even when you are wrong and outside God's perfect will. Look in the mirror before you point a finger because most of us have done it before. Some of us have argued back and forth and stubbornly stood when we knew we were wrong. We believed the longer we kept our position, the closer we would get to being right. To go a little farther, some of us had a "last man standing is the winner" mentality. We thought if we fussed and were stubborn enough, the other person would get tired, give up and give in. Then, their surrender would make us feel like we were right (although we were still wrong as plaids and polka dots on the same outfit). As we matured, many of us learned that if our point was not right and backed with *total* truth, it did not matter how hard we fought to prove it, our efforts were in vain.

Psalms 127:1 clearly says, "Except the Lord build a house, they labor in vain that build it." It's hard to misinterpret that. No matter how hard you try, how many years you stay together, how much public show you make to defend your error and image after you have started building a relationship with the wrong date or mate, that relationship you are trying to falsely preserve will not last. The biblical analogy of the wise man building his house on the rock while the foolish man built his house on sand makes it clear. It may exist for a moment, but it will soon fall down. He is the author and finisher of your faith, but you must follow the script of God, the solid rock, for your relationship to not only survive, but thrive as He intended.

The Lord has written the script for your entire life, but that does not mean you are automatically following what He wrote. As an actor or actress in His play, you are the one who chooses to follow His script or adlib. You adlib when you override His voice, ignore His signs and warnings and rush to do your own thing your own way. That's when you get off His script and onto your own. This does not only interrupt your life, but impacts the rest of the cast who are waiting for you to get back on God's script, His perfect will for you, so the play can roll as He planned.

You do not get punished and suffer needlessly when you stay with God's script. You do not negatively affect the other characters, alter their course or cause them confusion when you stay with His script. But like a good director, God will urge, nudge and encourage you to get you back on track and help you find your last line. When you get it right, He will continue rolling the film of your life from where you veered off His script, as if it never happened. Isn't that so amazing? Thank God for His grace and mercy!

Have you been following God's script or your own in relationships? Think about this. If you take the wrong exit when driving, how long do you continue in that direction once you realize you are off course? The farther you go the wrong way, the longer it may take, but the good news is, you can still arrive at your destination when you humble yourself and correct your error. The Lord desires to direct you to your destiny as you follow His lead. His vision for you is greater than you can imagine, but the only way you can get to an abundant love life is by following His script.

It was not God's plan for Adam and Eve's union or your relationship to be miserable, not advancing or progressing and going nowhere fast, but it will be when you are outside of His perfect will. When you do not listen to Him, you interrupt His perfect plan and cause yourself grief.

Father God really does know best, but sometimes we think we know better. We tell children to be obedient and follow their parents' instructions, yet, as adults we do not always follow Daddy's words of wisdom and direction. Just like you are looking out for a child's best interests because you can see down the road for his or her life, so is the Lord looking out for you. His goal is to spare you from avoidable drama, but you must listen! Too many adults are hard-headed children. As you may have already learned, you can save yourself so much pain and drama when you obey--do what Jesus tells you to *when* He tells you to do it.

God only planned a *perfect* will for your life. Contrary to popular belief, He is not the author of the term "permissive will." Truth is, you are either in God's perfect will or you are not. Because of His grace and mercy, He *permits* you to continue to live when you venture outside His perfect will, but He did not ordain or create a *permissive* will for you.

God also gave you a personal will, but it is in your best interest for your will to agree with His perfect will. The Bible's book of Jonah shows how serious God can be about getting you on track to His perfect will when you rebel and decide to do your own thing. You may not physically die, but God will make you cry out and surrender. Believe me. The most peaceful and happiest place to be is in God's will.

Exposing The Root Of Your Personal Drama

When we were children, my parents taught my sister and me a significant life lesson as they instructed us on how to beautify the flower beds that adorned our front yard. Our assignment was to pull out the weeds. First, they taught us how to distinguish the weeds from the growing flowers because before they bloom, some flower stems and weeds resemble. Second, mom and dad showed us how to successfully extract the weeds from the fertile soil.

At first, we pinched the tips of stringy, grass-like weeds and then attempted to yank them out of the soil. Patiently, mom and dad explained that if we only pulled the tip the weed would grow back; however, if we dug beneath the soil, pinched the weed's hidden white root and then pulled it up, that weed would not grow again. We listened and soon took great pride in our new job of "cleaning" the flower beds so the flowers could have more room to grow.

What our parents already knew and were teaching us was that when weeds are not dealt with and removed, they can overtake the flowers. In other words, the useless (weeds) would invade and overtake the useful (flowers). If you do not pull drama's unexposed roots out, it will show up in your life again. Your deliverance from drama begins by uprooting weeds that have grown alongside flowers in your heart's soil. When the roots are truly extracted, those weeds will not grow again. Exposing the root of past drama empowers you to change your future. Let's help you get delivered from drama by exposing and uprooting weeds that may have hindered your relationship success.

Internal Drama. *Do you see yourself as God sees you?*

God's true desire and will is for you to be wondrously happy, not eternally miserable in relationships. He knows that when you have low self-esteem and don't view yourself as He does, you may settle for less than His best in your dates and mates. People allow verbal, emotional, sexual or physical abuse when they have low self-esteem. They also allow financial abuse. An example of this is when single mothers on public assistance move their boyfriends in when it is not allowed on their leases or social service guidelines. If caught, they risk losing benefits and shelter for their children. Change your priorities ladies. Don't lose your soul or shelter for sex. If a man really loves you, he will not put you or the children at risk. God has blessed him with health and strength so he can work, get his home, marry you for the right reasons and make your life better. Do not compromise your self-worth any longer. Do not settle for less than a responsible, success-driven man!

God does not want any of His children to be abused and taken advantage of any longer. Domestic violence drama-- physical, verbal and emotional abuse are NOT okay. Married or not, run for your life if you are in that situation. Abusers are mentally deranged and many are capable of violent acts you cannot dream of. The news has been filled with too many reports of lovers brutally murdered by a violent, abusive partner. You have to stop abuse before your abuser destroys your self-esteem, your relationship with your family, your body or life. Victims should seek help! God's power is strong enough to free you from abuse.

A low sense of self-worth is the root of internal drama. People of all marital, social and financial statuses, races, genders, religions and educational levels struggle daily to overcome low self-esteem. Some doctors, lawyers, pastors, teachers, community leaders, business owners and stay-at-home moms battle it. Even celebrities who have millions of dollars and thousands of fans still feel insecure. As a result, many search to find meaning in their lives through violence, promiscuity, drug abuse, homosexuality, bad relationships and false religions. Yet they still feel troubled, lonely and empty. Looking for love in the wrong places, they soon discover that social approval alone will not fulfill you. Only knowing God's love will truly fulfill you.

Many people of all ages, including the well-educated, well-dressed and affluent, fight internal mental and emotional battles. Some wake up and insult the person they see in the mirror. They believe good things happen to everyone except them. They speak negative words over their lives like, "I am so unlucky and a failure." They compare themselves to other people who they think are better than they are and even become envious. Feeling unassured of their role in the Master's plan, their minds are filled with questions like, "*Am I cute enough, tall enough, slim enough, muscular enough, rich enough, educated enough or the right race or gender to be liked and accepted by people?*"

Maybe you have pondered those questions yourself. The truth is, God did a fantastic job purposefully creating you unique and beyond comparison. No other opinion matters when you know and believe what He says about you.

When you know who you are, who Jesus is, and what you can accomplish through Him, you can increase your self-worth and win the battle against low self esteem. Philippians 4:13 states, "I can do all things through Christ who strengthens me." Practically applied, that means unlimited possibilities and strength are flowing through your life when you are connected to Jesus Christ. He has the power to make you a real winner!

You can start the vital act of increasing your self-esteem right now in three easy steps--Read, Believe and Confess.
1) *Read* and learn what God said about you in the Bible. 2) *Believe* what He said about you. 3) *Confess* His words constantly. Repeat these over and over again until it sticks!

What has God said about you, His finest creation? You should *read, believe* and *confess* what the Bible says about you from Genesis to Revelations. These three scriptures that I have summarized lay a great foundation. Build on it.

Psalm 139:14 - You are fearfully and wonderfully made.
Genesis 1:27 - You are made in God's image and likeness.
Jeremiah 31:3 – God loves you with an everlasting love.

You are so special to God that He carefully designed you with precision and detail. Matthew 10:30 lets us know that He even knows the number of every single hair on your head, including the ones that have fallen out!

God has a divine purpose (a niche) which He designed you especially for. He planned to create you as you are, so stop comparing yourself to others and worrying about your complexion, voice, weight and height. Remind yourself that you are not inferior or superior to anyone else regardless of your race, marital, social or financial status. Stop feeling inadequate and unworthy of love because of past mistakes you made. God will not reject or give up on you because of those mistakes. His mercy endures forever. He still believes in you and has your bright future in mind.

When God first told the Biblical character Jeremiah that He had chosen him for special service, he was absolutely awestruck! Jeremiah felt so inadequate, inexperienced and unworthy. He was so young and felt far from perfect. Like you and I, he had stumbled a few times. Jeremiah was very likely tormented with the fear of what people would say and had a tendency to be easily swayed by their opinions.

But God already knew all of that about Jeremiah. He lovingly explained to him that before He formed him in his mother's womb, He already knew him and predestined him to be a prophet to the nations (Jeremiah 1:5). Later, in Jeremiah 29:11, God reinforced His great plans when He said through Jeremiah, "For I know the plans that I have for you, plans to prosper you and not harm you, to give you hope and a future, to give you an expected end." Despite your failures, God created you with purpose, too.

Before your mother met your father and his sperm slow-danced with her egg, God already knew you. I know it's hard if you feel abandoned by one or both of your parents, but do not waste more energy hating them. Thank them for doing one thing right. God used them to get you here. And like He had for Jeremiah, God has a plan for your life, too.

Getting to know God, your Creator, more is the only way you can truly get to know yourself better. You can go to others and ask them what they think you were created to do, but no one knows you like the One who made you.

When your vehicle needs servicing, the very best place to go is to the manufacturer's dealership. Why? Because they are highly specialized and have the most thorough knowledge of your vehicle's specific make, model and design, its custom features and how it was intended to function. You can go to a generic mechanic, but it's very possible that they may overlook or not detect all of your specific problems. Some mechanics intentionally create a new problem so that you have to go back to them again. (That's like confidants who give bad advice on purpose.)

God is our Manufacturer, so regardless of whether we only need a tune-up or a major system overhaul, He is the best person to consult since He knows every detail about how He made you. Going directly to God will save you the time, money, heartache and headache you get from consulting psychics, palm readers, horoscopes and dark sources when searching for true love in the wrong places.

You may have suffered past emotional, physical, or verbal abuse and put up with a lot of drama that you should not have while battling low self-esteem. You will only make true progress in life and love when you actively love God and yourself more. It doesn't matter to Him how great your social status, education, wealth or health is. His word applies to us all. Drawing closer to God draws you closer to your complete deliverance from internal drama.

Inherited Drama. *Your past may be influencing your present.*

Friend, Jesus loves you. Do you believe that He wants you to experience a better relationship than your family members have ever had? Do you believe He can do that for you? I do. But you must get delivered from *inherited* drama.

What kinds of relationships did you witness when you were growing up? Did you see genuinely loving married couples or the exact opposite? During childhood, many people saw poor relationship skills modeled in their households. Some parents, grandparents, aunts and uncles, cousins and friends lived in jacked up, dysfunctional relationships for years and tried to call them upright. Some lived together unmarried. Some were married to people who were verbally disrespectful, physically abusive, openly adulterous and emotionally disconnected or they were that way themselves. Some unmarried women were mistresses to married men. Other "role models" dabbled in witchcraft, participated in pornography, secretly molested children, practiced homosexuality and other perversities.

Who you are now is a partial product of your most familiar environment, your family. Most of your current viewpoints came from them. Reflect a minute on your life's relationship drama. Does your story resemble any of your closest relatives'? It's a big plus when you observed healthy, successful and spiritual marriages as a child. But as you now try to find your way to marital success as an adult, it can be quite a challenge to overcome and not repeat manipulative, detached, abusive, adulterous or other inappropriate relationships you witnessed as a child.

Examining your past is not an avenue to blame others. It's not to give you an excuse, but expose generational roots. When you understand the root of a problem you may be able to solve it, so let's deal with your crazy history and love life right now. You must pray for inherited drama to be uprooted and cooperate with God for deliverance before you can have a drama-free relationship. When He shows you how messed up you and those relatives were (and may still be), please pray for their deliverance, too.

Although your past may influence you to make wise or unwise choices in who you date and marry and how you handle marriage, you should not use poor past models as a copout for your own irresponsibility in striving to make your relationship work. Blaming all your mistakes on "not knowing any better" is not a sufficient excuse for adults. God has blessed you with too many opportunities to read, listen, improve and grow so you do not repeat the mistakes of your examples or the ones you previously made either.

Old familial mindsets can be stubborn and hard to break but they are not impossible to change. The enemy wants to keep you in your dreary past, but grab hold to God's better way. You constantly need to refresh yourself with new, valuable and life-giving information. You can retrain and renew your carnal mind to think and see like God does.

The great news is that the stronghold of generational curses can be broken with God's yoke destroying power. If your parents divorced or you are a divorcee, your children do not automatically have to marry and divorce. They can be blessed with successful marriages the first time around.

For lack of knowledge generations are destroyed and without vision people perish. You should have a future vision that is brighter than your past. Pray for the children. Use your tongue to speak life and hope into them and do not curse them. You be the one God uses to start the flow of generational relationship blessings into your family!

Proverbs 13:22 says a good man or woman leaves an inheritance for his or her children's children. So I ask you, what type of legacy are you leaving for your children and grandchildren? I'm not only speaking of money, real estate and personal property, but a legacy of godly family values.

What you do today can affect your family tomorrow. For those who hate the Lord, Genesis 20:5 says that the sins of the father can visit the child to the third and fourth generations. Does that make you think twice about some of the dirt you had planned to do? There is forgiveness when you ask for it. Choose to repent and leave a legacy of love.

"Father God in the name of Jesus, I repent and ask you to forgive me for my sins. I renounce any and all generational curses in my family (pride, rebellion, manipulation, selfishness, lust, abuse, treachery, lying, revelry, poverty, adultery, divorce) and speak generational blessings in Jesus name. I decree and declare that my family will not have to suffer the hardship, hurt and pain I've experienced because of foolishness, stubbornness, and refusing to obey your voice. May they be yielded and have tender hearts toward you. I ask that You order the steps of my children, cousins, nieces and nephews into their God-ordained mates so that their first marriages can be blessed. Help me to walk and live in Your great love so that I may leave a legacy of love. Amen."

Sexual Drama

Isn't it good to know future generations do not have to suffer as much as you have? You must help them avoid what may have been your worst setback--sexual drama.

Far too many unmarried couples, young and old, are jumping between the sheets way too soon. They have reduced the uniting, bonding, stimulating and erotic lovemaking God created exclusively for the marriage bed into a merely impulsive physical activity--in the school janitorial closet, in the back seat of a hidden vehicle, behind the bushes, in a secluded office, in a dorm room, bedroom or maybe in a hotel room--that no longer requires a committed relationship or true friendship. They try sex like they try on different pairs of shoes and switch partners like drivers switch lanes on the highway. As risky as sex is, some sexual partners barely even know each other's names.

The Bible, which is more relevant to everyday life than many think it is, truthfully states that some enjoy the "pleasures" of sin for a *season*. Seasons do change, so my question to you is, what happens when that "pleasure" is over? The physical sensation of having sex is pleasurable to the flesh, but having sex when you are unmarried is the sin called fornication. It's the sin of adultery when you have sex outside your marriage. A few minutes of pleasure, even with a "paid professional," can open gateways to pain greater and longer-lasting than the pleasure. You are aware of the physical consequences of diseases and pregnancy after sexual intercourse. But many people are unaware of its emotional and spiritual effect--the formation of soul ties.

When you make love with someone you form a strong unseen emotional bond with them. This is called a soul tie. You are supposed to have a good soul tie to your God-ordained mate, because it keeps you closely connected and wanting each other more and more. But sometimes, even with mates you self-select, you tie and tangle yourself through sexual intercourse to people that God did not predestine you to be with. Then you struggle with getting them completely out of your "system" although those ties are hindering your better future. (The Bible says the truth will make us free. Whew, that was tight, but it is right!)

When you are soul tied to people, you may act similar to them, think like them, and even encounter some of their same issues and challenges. Being soul tied to the wrong people or too many people negatively affects your emotional stability and can hinder your progression in life.

Examine yourself and think about these examples. If he or she has little zeal for life and low self esteem, do you find yourself fighting depression and low self esteem, too? Is he or she is indecisive and now you are, too? Have you changed and become willing to settle for less so you can be more comfortable with him or her and on his or her level?

If you get butterflies when an ex-lover calls and your mood suddenly changes, you are probably still soul tied. If you make love to one person while thinking about another, you are still soul tied. If you tried to rebound after a broken relationship but your next lover had the familiar spirit and personality as your last one, you were still soul tied to the old one though you thought you were moving on.

God intended for *godly* soul ties, ones from a loving and indisputably God-ordained relationship, to last forever. But you have to ask God to sever and free yourself from *ungodly* soul-ties, ones resulting from past relationships *you* chose. You likely know married and unmarried people who do not fully enjoy their present blessing because of ungodly soul ties to obnoxious and undeserving past dates and mates. Past intimacy created soul ties which have to be severed for them to fully move on. If you have had an affair or are divorced, you have to be sure to sever every ungodly soul tie with your ex. If not, you will put undue stress on your new relationship. The enemy will try to resurrect your disastrous past in your present relationship.

My Savior has power to deliver you from sexual drama! If you have had multiple sexual partners, you need to repent and verbally renounce every ungodly soul tie and ask God to sever them all. This prayer will help you.

Father God in the name of Jesus, this is your child _____ and I need your help. You know all about me. I ask you to forgive me of every impure thought and sexual sin I ever committed. Please forgive me from lust, fornication, adultery, masturbation, pornography and all illicit sexual acts I watched and committed. I did not realize what I was doing to my body, soul and spirit then and now I desire to please you. My flesh is weak so I need your strength. I plead the blood of Your Son Jesus over myself that my thoughts and my body might be pure so that I can present myself to You as a living sacrifice, holy and acceptable unto You which is my reasonable service as Romans 12:1 says. Help me to quickly cast down every wicked imagination and thought that the enemy sends to suggest for me to do what is displeasing to you. I ask You to sever every ungodly soul tie with people from my past and present so I can be empowered to embrace the bright future you have prepared for me. Burn up every tie with the fire of God so that I will never be entangled in those yokes of bondage again. I thank and praise you in advance for helping me to live holy so I can be pleasing in your sight. Help me do what I cannot do on my own. I ask this in the name of your precious Son Jesus. Amen.

More Sexual Drama

Premarital sex has been popularized by television, music and other media that promote sex as harmless, but it is not. You can lose your life's focus, contract diseases and become pregnant. Teenage pregnancy statistics are alarming. Abortion traumatizes women and is not birth control. AIDS and STDs are not all curable. Sex can be risky business!

God made males and females distinctly different. Many of our perceptions differ and so do our bodies. Men are physical first and emotional second. Women are emotional first, then physical. So when sex may be just a physical release and not much of an emotional encounter for an uncommitted man, a woman feels just the opposite. When she gives her body, she gives her all. It's emotional for her.

There are not many things worse than for a woman to give her precious pearls to a man and then he leave her, disrespect her and act like it meant nothing to him. Sadly, the formation of a soul tie leads her flesh to want to be intimate with him again despite his meanness. His rejection deeply hurts her because she gave him more than her body, she gave him her heart.

Then some women get trapped in wrong relationships, then try to use sex to keep men. She knows he is abusive and no good for her, but lust keeps her wanting him in her bed. Sex won't make grown men love you for real. Ladies, please love yourselves enough to let the wrong men go.

Many men have been led too long by the wrong head. They followed their penises, their feeling heads, when they should have used their brains, their thinking heads! Can I get an amen? Lack of self-control got them into trouble with a capital T. Their flesh was saying "yes" when it got a physical release, but many were soon arrested by a disease, an unplanned pregnancy, or a whole lot of drama after shooting a loaded, but unwrapped gun at the wrong target!

You only get God's results when you do things God's way. Save your heart trouble by not compromising! God instructs us not to have sex outside of marriage not as punishment, but divine protection. He created sex, so He knows all about its addictive pleasure and power. If you are a virgin, please continue to hold on and wait until you are married. Do not let anyone talk you out of your values of preserving your pearls for your mate. It will be worth it.

God wants you to enjoy guilt-free, unlimited, fulfilling and phenomenal lovemaking in His ordained marriage for you. So I must add this final note for the married. It does not quite make sense to be making less love now than when you were unmarried. Ouch! Neither is it God's will. So spouses, if you are not tending to one another's sexual needs, you, too, need to get delivered from sexual drama.

Same Sex Relationship Drama

Past molestation, abuse, bad heterosexual relationships, the desire to feel similarly comforted, understood and accepted, popularity, perversity, other issues and personal choices have resulted in people choosing to pursue same sex relationships. Homosexuality has experienced a heightened public awareness in recent years with the gay rights movement, increased political advocacy, same sex marriage being voted on in some states and more public display of homosexuality; however it existed millenniums ago. God called homosexuality a perversion then and despite public opinion, it is a perversion in His eyes now.

God made it clear in both the Old and New Testaments that homosexuality was more than just a sinful action, but an abomination--which means that it is disgusting, shameful, and detestable to Him. In Leviticus chapter 18, Moses reveals God's commands and specifically identifies improper sexual conducts to the children of Israel. In verse 22 he clearly instructs the men, "Thou shall not lie with mankind, as with womankind: it is abomination."

Here is a biblical illustration of how much God hates it. In Genesis 19:4-13, God sent male angels to help Lot escape God's destruction of Sodom for their grievous sins. The young and old Sodomite men saw them and surrounded Lot's house. They told Lot they wanted to "know" them. Lot offered his virgin daughters, but they did not want the women. They lusted after the men and almost broke Lot's door down to get to them! The angels rescued Lot, pulled him inside and smote the homosexual men with blindness.

God destroyed Sodom by fire as a consequence of their sins. He is more merciful today; however, homosexuality is still an unnatural passion. Experimenting with same sex relationships can lead to physical sickness and early death, but have you considered its consequence of spiritual death?

In I Corinthians 6:9-10, Apostle Paul admonishes the people not to be deceived because those who participate in homosexuality shall not possess the kingdom of God. In Romans 1:26-7, he tells the Romans how women exchanged their natural function for an unnatural and abnormal one, and men turned from natural relations with women and were set ablaze with lust for one another. The men, he said, committed shameful acts with men and suffered in their own bodies and personalities the inevitable consequences and penalty of their wrong-doing and going astray.

Have you ever thought of homosexuality as an insult to God since it contradicts His intended purpose? God created men and women's genitals complementary, like a lock and key, for maximum fulfillment for husband and wife. Anal, oral and vaginal sex using toys are NOT godly behaviors between two born males or two born females.

Contemporary culture has popularized homosexuality and bisexuality. I am especially concerned about the impact of this influence on our youth, college students and young adults. Homosexual spirits have slipped into the church, too. Now you have firm biblical reasons to say "no" if you are tempted. If you have tried it already, please repent and ask the Lord's help. He hates the sin of homosexuality, but He loves sinners enough to deliver them from that drama.

Christianity and Your Relationship History

How does Christianity impact relationship success? If you want to have *love without the drama*, I suggest you get to know Jesus Christ as your personal Lord and savior. He is the One who set the example of true love when He forgave others and willingly sacrificed His life for the whole world. Many have heard about Him, but fewer truly know Him.

It is important to note that a person can be a church member, leader or employee and still have to overcome the challenges of flawed relationships. Every individual has a historical database of ideas about relationships that heavily influences his or her definition of love and the components of a successful relationship. This familiar definition of love is based on prior personal experience, biblical and non-biblical teachings, family teaching and the demonstrations of others they closely watched during dating and marriage.

When you surrender your life to Christ, your spirit becomes new; however, your old ideas about relationships do not automatically become purified and godly. Your mind must be transformed and renewed daily. The ideas which do not agree with God's principles must be moved out by studying the truth, fasting, prayer and practice. That territory must be reoccupied with God's truth about love.

The church is a hospital, so do not assume everyone you meet in church is healed. You have to carefully examine people you meet there to see if they are spiritual doctors, nurses, patients or visitors. Don't judge or give up on a person in church who has been divorced either. Their past is the past, but God promises them a much brighter future!

Deliver Me From Drama.

The climbs, twists, turns, dips, drops and upside down moments riding on the relationship rollercoaster have been a thrill for some and have left others with upset stomachs. However you feel, do not give up on love completely--just give up on loving your old way and start loving God's way. Friends, family and others may act like they know everything about love, but their influence and opinions can cause you drama, too. God is the only One who can truly lead you to experience and enjoy *love without the drama.*

Positive points can be found in your negative past experiences. As you seek God and grow in Him more, He will illuminate errors you made and show you where you missed His mark so that you do not blindly repeat the same mistakes again. So many people feel totally condemned because of their past errors, but thank God for His amazing grace and mercy. Confess to God, stop fearing people, be truthful and stop hurting yourself and others because you were wrong when you wanted to be right. The good news is our Lord is not just God of a second chance, but many chances! It is God's truth and not man's opinions that matter at the end of the day--and for eternity, too.

Many people have issues within themselves that they need to examine and address before they cast stones at everyone else's relationship foibles and failures. Matthew 7:3-5 and Luke 6:41-42 say to first cast the small particle out of your own eye and then you can see clearly to cast the beam out of your brother's eye. That's why this chapter was all about *you* getting delivered from drama first.

It is dangerous when people live in dysfunction so long that they get used to it and begin to think that misery is part of every relationship. Most who think like that have wrecked love lives today. Bound by low self-esteem and others' opinions, they live beneath God's privileges in love.

Humans make mistakes; however, that is not a license to live and love recklessly. If you are married, there's no time like the present to let go of self and let God have His way in love. If you are unmarried, take all the time you need to get delivered from drama before you date and seek a mate. Whether your personal drama is petty or drastic, you will not have a drama-free relationship until it is dealt with.

It is insanity to continue to handle relationships the same way and expect different results. Perhaps you have never examined the word of God to see what words of life it has to help you have truly blessed relationships, so let me lead the way. God's word shows us the way to love ourselves better so we can love others on His level, but if we never open it, we will not know what He has to offer us. So submit yourself totally to Him, listen and learn so you and your love life can be delivered from drama.

Will you believe with me that God can make your future romance more like smooth sailing than a rollercoaster ride? If you are tired of the results of doing relationships your way and have never tried relationships God's way, now is the time to try Him. If you already know Jesus as your savior, why not give Him total control and let Him navigate your romantic relationships, too? That, my friend, is the only way for you to have *love without the drama*.

CHAPTER TWO
Love Games

If you want to play games, play Monopoly. Don't play with love.
- Lynetta Jordan

Do you have any ex-lovers that deserve an Oscar or Emmy award for their dramatic performances in your life? Some played the roles of genuinely caring persons so well that they fooled you. But like many movie stars, they were motivated by money, opportunity and fringe benefits. They saw an opportunity to be seen, be funded and reap the benefits of celebrity status and being treated like royalty with you. Like actors, they intrigued you with dramatic presentations, but avoided the attachment of their hearts. The sweet words they recited were a rehearsed script. When the movie was over and they got what they wanted, they disappeared off the scene of your life. Oh what pain!

People are to be appreciated, not played with. Romantic relationships are serious matters of the heart, not games for mere challenge or entertainment. It is dangerous to mishandle someone's emotions. Some immature, selfish adults play childish relationship games; however, they should heed the following warning. Undermining any relationship is a good way to cancel hope of lasting success in the relationship you want to succeed the most.

I hope you have not been the game's culprit! When you thought you were it--a little younger, slimmer, more hair-- you may have played some terrible games on unsuspecting dates and mates! Before you can realize your dream, you must do away with all evil motives and those deceptive egotistical games you played on dates "back in the day."

Getting "played" in love hurts deeply, but God is a healer. At some point in life, even the best of us have been mishandled by a player who treated love like a pointless game with no true winner. In the love game, one person leads another to believe he or she is the object of the other's affection, but they are really the object of the other's game. Haven't you met someone who you thought had the same motives and intentions as you, but after you were in pretty deep, you discovered that their motives and intentions were distinctly different? Being a fool in love who ends up being fooled by what you thought was love can make you feel pretty low. But life isn't over. God can restore your joy.

Players, who can be male or female, are selfish opportunists with little heart. Most aim to take advantage of another's vulnerability, weakness and genuine desire for true love. Players see a date or mate as an opportunity to bring sexual, social or financial gain to their own lives. Some get an evil thrill seeing how many people they can trick or manipulate into thinking that their love is genuine. Other players lay their cards out on the table, tell prospects their games and wait for them to take heed to their warnings and dump them. When you tolerate their games, most players consider that as permission to disrespect you.

Discerning Players And Their Love Games

When you become more spirit-led than flesh-led you will be better equipped to discern players and their games. Your flesh can lead you to mingle with people who are not compatible with your spirit. What your eyes behold can mesmerize you so much that you forget to look through the eyes of the spirit to examine a man or woman's character. Human nature gives the sexy "the benefit of the doubt." A woman's sweet voice, shapely curves and voluptuous breasts can give a man temporary amnesia and almost make him forget his own name. A man's good looks, deep voice, ripped chest, smooth skin and pretty white teeth can make a woman's heart flutter and mouth stutter when she talks. Evaluating character based on your flesh's initial reaction will get you in trouble so deep that you need a savior, the Savior, to rescue you! You know that's the truth.

Galatians 5:16 says that when you walk according to the spirit, you will not fulfill the lusts of the flesh. That is your protection against being tricked and trapped by love games so easily. It can be hard to discern if you are the object of a love game initially. For example, some men act interested, but their ulterior motive is to see just how close they can get to making a good girl go bad and have premarital or extramarital sex. Some gold digging women pretend to love men just so they can receive financial dividends and benefits. When the money stops flowing, so does their shallow love. That's why you have to watch *and* pray.

People commonly assume that prospective dates and mates have the same motives and standards as them, but not always. If you do what appears to be right with the wrong motive, that is sin. Remind yourself that everyone does not handle relationships with honesty and respect.

Noone discloses everything when you first meet. After you move past the initial physical attraction, you must spend quality time with a person and carefully observe his or her conversations, mannerisms, attitudes and reactions toward you and others in family, friend, professional and social situations over a period of time to truly learn his or her ways. Even then, some bipolar dates or mates skillfully perform like actors who live for curtain call.

Take your time and walk, not run when pursuing your next relationship. If you are presently single, become a God chaser while you wait for love to manifest. While waiting, focus on building your confidence in the Lord and self-improvement. When you love God and yourself well, it will not be easy for an ill-motived lover to trick or trap you.

Men can see and smell when a woman is weak, lacks confidence and is most vulnerable to fall prey to a game. When a man who does not consider himself accountable to Christ perceives a woman is emotionally needy, she may be a prime candidate for his game. That serpent will say the right things with the goal of slithering straight into her bed.

Loving God and you more will decrease your chances of getting "played" in a love game. Get delivered from codependency. Never make anyone your total focus and lose yourself in them. Improve numero uno! Set goals and work toward them. Participate in positive activities like church, children's lives or book clubs. Live, laugh and love!

The Dating Game

I recall watching a favorite show, The Dating Game, when growing up. In thirty minutes minus commercials, a male or female had to ask questions of three potential dates and select the one he or she believed to be most compatible. As viewers of the tube, we saw the top choice at the end of each show, but we rarely heard the rest of their stories or if they found true love at all. Now that I think about it, was that sufficient time to ask enough questions to determine if anyone would be a suitable date? Or was the entertaining show just an effort to earn top television ratings after all?

The twenty-first century has presented new avenues to seek and find dates. Television and the world wide web are flooded with reality dating shows. Social networking sites have experienced exponential growth. Free and fee-based online dating services abound and some have enhanced their credibility with compatibility questionnaires. Now registered users are not limited to selecting local dates. They can mingle with potential dates from across the USA.

With such random methods to search for true love, you can sign up for a date with destiny or a date with the devil. The danger of the dating game is that all people do not deal fairly. Some lie about their names, ages and other pertinent details. They only tell you what they want you to know.

You do not have to accept any invitation immediately. It is wise to pray (and wait for God's answer) about anyone who desires to date you since the devil sends dates, too. When you let God choose your dates and mate, you can eliminate a lot of love games and dating disappointment.

What you don't know won't hurt you. Or will it?

One of my all-time favorite movies is *Perfect Holiday*. It is a beautiful love story with a great ending; however, at the beginning, one of the main characters employed as Santa's elf, lied about his occupation. He was dishonest because he feared that the object of his affection would reject him if he told the truth. A date may take great measures to impress you, but like this character, it may not be the truth.

"What you don't know won't hurt you," is a popular cliché that is dangerously far from the truth. (Men, what page is that phrase on in the official player's manual?) What many of us did not know, but later found out about an ex or the person we are with now has probably hurt us most. What you didn't know about him or her *then* can be a source of your heartache and pain *now*. Can I get an amen?

Perhaps you now realize that lust and what you thought was love blinded you. From past experience you now know that a hurting heart definitely does not help you see or think straight. Understanding the purpose and value of lessons learned can help you forgive yourself for making bad relationship decisions. Thinking on that too long can lead to the depressing "shoulda, coulda, wouldas," so please do not torment yourself by focusing on it much more. So if you hooked up with Mr. or Miss Wrong instead of Mr. or Miss Right when you were on the rebound, forgive yourself for ignoring, missing, or overlooking what you needed to see in the new date or mate and for making the wrong decision so quickly. Then wise up. Do not be so anxious and do not ignore God's red flags the next time!

The Sex Game: *Lust versus Love*

You can also avoid being played when you refuse to compromise God's standards for sexual purity. *Love* and *lust* are two four letter words that get confused quite a bit. In a world where morals seem to be getting looser by the day, women and men have to be more discerning than ever of the motives of people they meet. Too many times people who say they love you are not sincere. Personally, I would rather someone be truthful and plainly state, "I'll act like I love you as long as I get what I want," than attempt to fool me into thinking that they care. How about you?

Men who have promiscuous pasts and pride themselves in their sexual performances often think they know everything it takes to satisfy a princess, but even some of them have been tricked. You and I both know men who have been blindsided by evil, treacherous women as a result of prioritizing fleshly fantasies and second-guessing good advice, observation and intuition. After being left with a big hole in their hearts, feeling a deep void and longing for true emotional fulfillment, they also discovered that the physical stimulation of sexual escapades alone is not enough for a totally satisfying relationship.

Crafty "lovers" employ manipulative words and deeds to deceive unsuspecting partners into believing they are in love with them when actually, they are lusting after their physical bodies, money, clout or social statuses. How many ladies have been fooled by dates who said they loved them as part of their masterplans to gain their confidence and weaken them until they surrendered their priceless pearls?

After obtaining the desired precious prize, that Romeo disappeared into the night or may have left her laying there in the morning. The painful aftermath may have included emotional distress, public and private disrespect from him and others, a sexually transmitted disease or pregnancy. Some women even chose abortions as they were abandoned to walk through pregnancy alone. So if you have been wondering why he or she stopped calling after they made love to you, it really wasn't l-o-v-e. It was l-u-s-t. Let's clear the confusion. *Lust* is not the same as *love*.

How can you say *love* someone and then suddenly not want to talk to them anymore forever? Love will not allow you to do that (except briefly when an emotionally overwhelmed, head over heels in love macho man is trying to calm his wildly pulsating heart), but with selfish lust it's easy to do. After a lustful person gets your goodies, he or she no longer seeks to give you real love straight from the heart. When you emerge from under a players' covers, your nakedness *and* their true motives are also uncovered. It's a hard blow when you find out that a player only pretended to love you to get you between the sheets. After physically seducing your body, he or she left you with a broken heart.

After giving love your best shot, you may have been left emotionally depleted when you realized that the one you thought loved you really only lusted after you. I've heard lustful males make comments like, "All private parts are the same. It doesn't matter what she looks like in the dark." The truth, "I'm lusting after you," sounds cold-hearted, but wouldn't life be less painful if people told the truth?

The Truth About Lust

The Lord empowered and blessed me to demonstrate integrity among students on campus my entire four years of undergraduate education at Elizabeth City State University (ECSU). To God be the glory, His light shined amidst temptations galore! While there, God favored and honored me to be chosen by my peers to reign as campus queen, Miss ECSU, and be featured in Ebony magazine. Now who said you could not serve God and be popular?

As queen, I enjoyed conversating with athletes, sorority and fraternity members and other students on campus daily. Many of them complimented my godly standard. They had never heard my name as the victim of a train run or seen my face at any drug and sex-laced parties. I was friendly to everyone and never ran any man down or acted like a sports groupie who would do any illicit act to be seen with an athlete. I want to let you in on a secret those young men shared with me. They told me, "Lynn, we will sleep with any girl who wants to give it up. But when we want to settle down, we don't choose those girls. We go after the girls who have not given their bodies to everybody."

Now that may seem crazy for guys who were sleeping around to say, but they made a point. The truth about lust came straight from the mouth of men who may have been guilty of it. Lust (fulfilling physical pleasures) is a different ballgame than love (having an emotional commitment and connection). If you spend too much time on lust, you can miss out on love. Listen ladies. If you want to be respected, do not have sex to get men to like you. It will backfire.

The Danger Of Having Sex Too Soon

Let's keep it real. You don't have to search for sexual temptation because temptation is already on the prowl for you. You may have fallen head over heels in lust that you thought was love before. Even with good intentions to stay sexually pure, you may have grasped a personal revelation of Matthew 26:41, "The spirit is willing, but the flesh is weak." If you have fallen sexually, it is time to get back up.

You must die to the flesh if you want to truly live. Despite what many believe, God did not give the "no sex outside of marriage rule" because He wanted to spoil your fun and make you have a boring life with one partner only. Premarital and extramarital sexual relations have led to the downfall of countless relationships. Having sex too soon is dangerous and causes you to lose fellowship with God.

Since God invented sex, don't you think He knew the effect its thrill, feel and emotions would have on you? Sex is a highly addictive physical act with heavy emotional repercussions. Having sex ties you and your partner and naturally makes you yearn to be with them more in most cases. However, sex can be deceiving when the man perceives it as physical, but to the woman it is emotional.

God designed sexual pleasure to be desirable, but that's not the complete definition. He created sexual intercourse for enjoyment and procreation *in marriage only*. Having sex outside of marriage is sin. Sin separates us from God and causes spiritual decline. The more you have sex outside your marriage, the farther apart from God you will grow. But you are never too far to come back home to Him.

Compromise Is Not Worth It.

Our hearts drop in disappointment when awakened to the fact that compromising morals, the value and virtue of our bodies to a man or woman whose sentiments are not sincere, is never worth it. Reflect on your past. How many relationship failures did it take for you to realize that?

For your benefit and His pleasure, God wants you to follow I Corinthians 6:18 and flee fornication and adultery. I've heard too many people in church attempt to exempt themselves from God's directives by saying, "God knows how I am," or a similar excuse. No matter if he or she is a musician, deacon or officer, a person who talks like that is not fully submitted and surrendered to God. I call them "*ain'ts*", not saints, as they are missing the supernatural "S" on their chests. Flesh-led, they stubbornly refuse to make an honest effort to abstain from sex out of season to please the God they say they love. These persons do not set good examples. It takes Jesus, but you can be kept. God knows you are not perfect yet, but you should definitely be trying!

The frailty of flesh is very real, but that is no excuse to stop working on mortifying its deeds as Romans 8:13 says. We all have sinned and come short of God's glory whether in our thoughts, words or deeds in the past, but with Christ we have power to break out of sin's chains. Apostle Paul acknowledged his everyday effort to honor God when he said, "I die daily." Every single day we must persevere to live holy. If you are better now than you used to be, praise God and continue to press toward perfection. He sees your efforts and He rewards those who diligently seek Him!

If you ever thought you could make someone genuinely love you by giving them sex, you were dead wrong. Have you ever exhausted yourself trying to earn love from lovers you could not please no matter how hard you tried? You compromised everything you believed in to make them happy, but you could never do enough. They stayed upset, found fault and blamed you for not giving them reasons to love you more. When you wanted an item, they would hold the carrot in your face, but as soon as you reached, they pulled it back or had you play another game to get it. That was emotional abuse. That is miserably frustrating.

You may have yielded and had sex outside of marriage expecting to receive real love in return, but it puzzled you when the opposite happened. Instead of being treated better, you were rejected and treated worse. The enemy and lustful flesh are never satisfied. The devil laughs when Christians compromise with him, so don't you be his fool.

You can avoid many pitfalls and lots of drama when you do not compromise God's sexual guidelines. Many women think sexual compromise encourages a man to show them pure love and respect in return. Not so! Premarital sex often has the opposite effect. You risk that person also verbally, physically and socially disrespecting you.

Ladies listen, if you want a man to commit to you, do not compromise. Whatever you compromise to keep, you will lose. When you think sex is keeping his love, you are losing his respect. It is depressing to discover that after you have given him your precious pearls, there's a great chance he may not be motivated to marry you. Avoid that drama!

The Cohabiting Game

Living together unmarried is the enemy's copout and counterfeit for marriage. Older generations called it shacking up. Genesis 2:24 states that a man shall leave his father and mother and cleave unto his *wife*. It does not say *girlfriend*. In some families it has been acceptable, almost a tradition for couples to live together while unmarried. It may seem convenient, but cohabiting dishonors God.

Cohabiting lacks the commitment God expects. It makes it easier for a person *not* to marry you since they get many marriage benefits without commitment. Haven't you heard the phrase, "Why buy the cow when you can get the milk for free?" Nowadays people give the milk *and* meat away freely. When the valuable parts are free, that doesn't leave much incentive to buy the cow. Prove you value yourself by not giving up your milk and meat prior to purchase!

Quite a few people have suffered great disappointment after spending years living with someone while expecting to receive a return on their investment, a future marriage. Even when cohabiting couples eventually marry, statistics show higher divorce rates for them. Time is precious and the older you get, the more precious it is. Once you know in your heart that a person you live with is not your true mate, why spend more years with them? If this is you, fight fear and stop settling so you can get who God has for you.

If you are dating now, have conversations about habits, expectations and household management before marriage, but wait until you marry to live together. It's simple. If you are not ready to marry, you should not cohabit either.

The Extramarital Game

Let me expose a big myth right now. Marriage papers won't change a player. Unfortunately, the legal marriage commitment is not powerful enough to undo and uproot a lustful spirit in anybody. Deliverance from adultery can only be achieved through repentance, submission and intentional cooperation with God's word and spirit.

Cheating spouses often play the blame game. They draw victims with stories of how bad they are treated at home. They often talk terribly about their spouses to get everyone to side with them and justify their lack of self-control. Ask yourself, "If life at home is so bad, why are they still there?" That will help you dismiss the lies of a cheater.

Extramarital affairs may be games to their players, but they are serious. Exodus 20:14, "Thou shalt not commit adultery," is one of the Ten Commandments. Any "benefit" a mistress or mister may receive is no match to God's punishment. Adultery, which can be between two married persons who are not married to each other or a married and unmarried person, can lead to family heartbreak, too.

If you know you will cheat when you are married, wait until you are more mature to commit. Matthew 5:32, Matthew 19:9 and Mark 10:4 allude to sexual unfaithfulness being biblical grounds for divorce. The adultery game can backfire. The guilty can lose it all, even real love in divorce.

God still forgives adulterers. In John 8, Jesus forgave a woman brought to Him by men who caught her in the act. The law said to stone her, but Jesus let her go and told her to sin no more. If you have been guilty, go and sin no more!

Players And The Game

So how do you get the strength to let go of the wrong relationship when you have been holding on to it for so long? The answer is...love yourself enough to tell the truth and reevaluate your relationship. One simple technique that helped me do that was what I call, "Doing the math."

Whether you feel your love relationship is good or bad, why don't you try "doing the math" now? Visualizing the abundance or lack of love you have been receiving will help you see how balanced your "give and take" really is. It will also show you areas of improvement or help you see what everyone else may have been trying to tell you, that someone is being played and your love is off balance!

Take a sheet of paper and draw a line down the middle. Write your name at the top of the left side and your love's name on the top right. List your positive contributions to your relationship. Then list his or hers. Next, take the time to list each others' spiritual, financial, social and emotional benefits of being in this relationship. It is understandable that contributions can shift during times of hardship, but take careful notes, because to have *love without the drama*, nobody should be giving extremely more than they are receiving all of the time. Review the results. If you are on the losing side--constantly giving more than you receive--you may need to let that burdensome relationship go.

It's sad that some lovers are users who want something in return for giving little or nothing of sacrificial value. Undisciplined lovers who are living outside of conviction will go as far as you let them. They will sweet talk, deceive and make promises they have no plans to keep in order to get what they want from you while minimally contributing to your support and emotional health. Your flesh will war against your spirit when you realize it is time to let them go, but you must put a stop to their antics by refusing to be used any longer.

You can let go of the wrong relationship with God on your side! Your love for yourself, our awesome God and the desire not to displease and disappoint Him should make you want to leave Delilah alone so you can have your destined Proverbs 31 woman, men! Ladies, love yourself enough to drop Bozo to make room for your God-ordained Boaz and all the blessings He will bring to your life!

Since Satan can disguise himself as an angel of light, you need Holy Spirit to help you discern potential dates and mates. The devil wants you to forfeit your true destiny. He cannot take away the relationship God has prepared for you. However, the enemy can try to get you off track and frustrate you so bad that you give up too soon or get out of position to receive your dream. Satan will always present a trick with hopes of keeping you away from God's treat. He or she will have many traits you desire, but something significant will always be missing. When you realize that he or she is not it, don't just stay in a mess. Exit the stage!

I hope "doing the math" will help strengthen you to be delivered from unbeneficial, dead end relationships, too. When your heart is right before the Lord, He will contend with the players who tried to play their love games on you. So let go, let God and experience *love without the drama!*

CHAPTER THREE

Heal Me From Heartbreak
Am I Bitter or Better?

When you are truly tired of the way things are, you will make a change and no longer wait for a change. Be the change you desire.
- Lynetta Jordan

Are you ready for your dream relationship right now? If you are still bitter, resentful or secretly or openly harboring unforgiveness toward anyone in your heart--ex-lovers, others or yourself, you are not quite ready yet. Letting go of past pain is necessary as you prepare to handle the blessing of a new, drama-free relationship. So let's start the journey to help you heal from past relationship wounds.

Jesus has the power to transform your past misery into future ministry! Are you wrestling with overcoming a past heartbreak? Do you host daily pity parties because of love once lost? God sees and cares. You don't need a psychic or horoscope to forecast your future. Jesus, *the* best emotional healer I know, wants to lead you to a better future.

Psalms 147:3 says, "The Lord heals the brokenhearted and binds up all their wounds." That written promise is for you. Receive it. His words on these pages have potential and power to help you heal from heartbreak and forgive. You do not have to remain bitter. You can become better!

My prayer is that as you turn these pages, you will be set free from the pain and drama of your past and shed the weight of any past hurt, bitterness, unforgiveness, envy or resentment that you are still holding on to. Through the burden-removing, yoke-destroying power of Jesus Christ, you can experience emotional healing, inner strengthening and a heartfelt release from all of your past emotional pain.

Depending on how severe your pain, the healing power of God may sound too good to be true, but it is not. My dear friend, I know it is real. How do I know so well? I am a living testimony of His emotional healing power. He healed my broken heart and wounded emotions more than once. Today I am walking, living and loving in His victory.

God brought me out of unhealthy, dead end drama where I held on to "potential" for years, then finally woke to reality. I could not change this man who had a divine call, but refused to surrender to God's will and chose to pursue the world. Later, I personally experienced God's reviving power again when Satan's deception interfered with the relationship blessing I had been praying, waiting and believing for--a gentle, good and most importantly, a man who loved God and me and demonstrated the very essence of God's extravagant love, the flow of Song of Solomon type love that literally "takes your breath away." Our dream relationship was invaded by lies, dream killers and destiny stealers and left for dead--brutally sabotaged by envious enemies cleverly disguised as spiritual friends I worshipped with. David expressed my sorrow in Psalms 55:12-14, 20-21. Read it. Only Jesus could heal me after that!

That was the time in my life when I discovered firsthand that grief caused by the disappointment, betrayal and deceptive actions of living persons can be more intense than grief caused by the death of someone you dearly love. But in the days that followed, God revealed His emotional healing power like never before. He relocated my mind from constant bombardment of painful thoughts to a place of peace and rest as I learned to let go, cast my cares on Him and trust Him to avenge my dream's slaughterers. He encouraged and helped me wait patiently on His promised power to show up and resurrect this Lazarus-like situation.

God's spirit rushed in like a flood to remind me of Isaiah 54:17, that no weapon formed against me shall prosper, even though it looked and felt like the intended weapons had worked. He reassured me that His perfect will would be accomplished, that what He had spoken was forever settled and that everything He promised was coming to pass. As I gave vengeance to Him, He helped me forgive those enemies, which released me from the pounding pain.

My journey was not all about me. I had to endure all of that to be a tried, tested and qualified encourager today. I want you to be so restored after your heartache that you, too, will one day be able to offer powerful words of hope and healing to someone who is presently experiencing what you have successfully endured. You may be so distraught right now that you cannot envision encouraging anybody, but when God performs His work and heals your broken heart after you wondered if you would ever be whole again, you will not be able to contain your joy either!

Heal Me From Heartbreak

When I experienced the devastating heartbreak of a broken relationship, the Lord healed, restored and revived me as I journeyed through these three significant steps:

(1) Acknowledge your pain.

(2) Allow yourself to grieve.

(3) Choose to forgive.

Let us examine each step as we progress toward your manifestation of total healing from a broken heart, too.

Acknowledge Your Pain. *"I'm hurting and I want to be healed."*

When you first experience anguish after a broken relationship, it feels like that agonizing pain will not cease. Its pangs are sharp and shocking. Its grief is grueling and gloomy. But beloved, trouble does not last always.

"This, too, shall pass," was one of my mother's favorite scriptures. Have you ever known any atmospheric storm to last forever? The sight and sound of a brilliant, booming and blustery thunderstorm may be fierce, but it is short-lived. Storms don't stay. They soon pass. Your emotional storm will subside, too. You can survive life's passing storms when you expect them to end and have faith that the sun will shine again. And you must not forget--it takes the sun, rain and storm clouds to create a radiant rainbow.

If you are hurting right now, confessing the truth will help lift your load. Even if you do not tell one person that your heart is bleeding, you must honestly confess the truth to God. He already knows, but you will not see His mighty deliverance manifest until *you* humbly admit the truth.

Foolish pride will hinder and delay you from admitting to your misery, but confession is beneficial and so good for your soul. True confession requires that you be brutally honest with yourself and God. Though your sin makes you feel naked before Him, you do not have to be ashamed because He knew you before you knew yourself. He will clothe you again with His righteousness when you admit the truth. He already knows everything you did, all the reasons why you did it and how much you avoided and ignored His voice when He told you not to do it. So what makes you think you are hiding anything from Him?

For every effect there is a cause. As you honestly confess and acknowledge your pain, it is utterly important that you own up to your part of the relationship's issues. Assess your companion's role in the situation, but as you do that, examine your role to its demise, too. It is easy to angrily blame everything on him or her--especially when you are embarrassed--but have you considered that God may have allowed that shame so you would look in His mirror?

You may think you are one hair away from perfection, but it is possible that your own actions landed you in this broken place. Ask, *"Was the break-up an attack against a God-ordained relationship by our trembling enemy who knows that an equally yoked couple on one accord can tear his kingdom down? Did the plan I mapped out--which I realize was not God's perfect plan--backfire? Am I reaping the pain from rebellion, selfishness and refusing to listen to truth?"* God won't tell your business when you ask Him what you did wrong. When He shows you, correct it quickly and do not repeat that drama again!

Don't let the pain you felt be wasted. Gain from your pain.

Painful lessons are powerful lessons. You seldom forget what heartbreak teaches you. In some cases of love lost, you may have been a victim of unfaithfulness, rejection, betrayal or emotional or physical abuse by your love interest. That pain was not your fault. But you should now be mature enough to honestly examine whether or not any of your own wrong motives, hardheadedness, bad personal decisions and choices were a source of heartache, grief and disappointment in past and present relationships, too.

Think about it. When you were younger, you could blame others and attribute some wrong date and mate choices to what you had not yet learned to look for, listen for and expect from the opposite sex. Though still learning, you are older and hopefully now more mature. What has pain taught you that will help prevent future heartbreak? In what specific ways might you change future dating practices (or encourage single persons in your sphere of influence) so that heartache like yours will not be repeated?

Regardless of whether someone else caused your heart to bleed or you are suffering from a self-inflicted wound, if you are still hurting, you can start the healing process by taking the first step of acknowledging your pain. Acknowledge your pain to God in prayer. Tell Him all about it. God loves you more than you can imagine, so you don't have to fear him rejecting or ridiculing your heartfelt words like an ex-lover may have. God stays in love with you, even while He gently waits for you to humble yourself and confess your faults before He fixes many situations.

Prayer, communicating and fellowshipping with God, is designed to be an intimate two way conversation. It does not matter if you are an experienced prayer warrior or a new believer praying for the first time. God is listening and longs to hear from you. You can start your prayer by expressing how much you love and appreciate God. Thank and praise Him for breathing life into you, your family, putting encouragement on your path, and providing life's necessities of food, shelter and clothing for you. Ask for His forgiveness for any sin you committed in word, thought or deed. Ask for His wisdom and request His help. Pour out your heart and release the heavy burdens as you tell Him exactly how you feel. Then bask in His presence, listen with your heart and wait for His answers or a sense of peace, even if it takes more than a few minutes.

God wants you to pray about everything and you can pray everywhere. You do not have to be in a church or synagogue on the Sabbath Day to pray. You can pray on your knees, walking around, while sitting, driving or even laying down. You can pray in the car, at home, on your job or while walking down the meat aisle in the grocery store. Just pray and know that God will meet you wherever you are when you call upon His name and ask for His help.

Jesus is always listening to your heartfelt cries. Not everyone understands your pain like He does. Heartbreak can lay you prostrate in a pool of tears, but He will come to you. The human touch is desirable, but when you cannot find a friend, God is there. He won't tell your secrets either. Have you tried talking to God yet? Now is the perfect time.

Allow Yourself To Grieve. *"I am grieving, yet I am grateful."*

Have you ever felt like your heart was ripped down the middle or snatched right out of your chest when the one you loved abused, cheated, broke up with, left, divorced or got married on you? You may not understand why you hurt so bad as the paralyzing shock froze your hopes and dreams, left you speechless, and possibly in an angry rage. What may have surprised you more was that as the initial shock died, the pain still lingered. That's when grief began.

Grief is a necessary but uncomfortable period of time of transition when you mentally deal with new realities you suddenly have to face after a tragic blow. During grief you outwardly express your sorrow to help purge and relieve intense inner pain. Grief's anguish is so strong that you must let it out so it will not damage or depress your mind. Do not attempt to bottle uncontainable emotions inside.

If you avoid grieving, you will delay your healing. Society sometimes insinuates that we are weak when we cry, but God gave us tears to help us grieve. Some women and men feel like they have to be so strong that they are not allowed to grieve. Let me correct them. It is healthy to grieve. We *must* all process our pain in order for wounded emotions to fully heal. Grief can make grown men wail like wet babies, but do not let that scare you. Grieving does not show that you are weak; it confirms that you are human.

Listen. Life is not over when someone hurts you. The sooner you allow yourself to grieve your loss, the sooner you can get your life back. From personal experience I know you can make it through and be ready to love again.

I felt like a single victim of double murder when an envious longtime "friend" endeavored to destroy a priceless new and growing friendship I had commenced with a phenomenal, hard-working, God-loving man. The exposure of this evil attempt to assassinate our characters and betray trust and confidence instantly annihilated the friendship I thought I had with her. The blow I felt when her cunning deception--likely aimed to murder my joyful relationship with him--sent his and my targeted friendship-relationship directly into intensive care hurt so much more! This atrocity was like two gunshot wounds to my heart. Shocked and surprised at such an evil deed and its damaging effects, I was thrown into instant grief. Almost breathless, I needed emotional resuscitation as I suddenly found myself gasping for air, peace and consolation as I cried buckets of tears alone in life's emergency room.

This was the time when I realized that grief caused by people who are living can be worse than grief over the dead. I had grieved my grandfather's sudden death, but that did not compare to the grief my new friend and I suffered after exposure of the lies, deceitful deeds and discord sown by a woman I once called a sister. It is hard to explain the devastation, hurt and sorrow we felt when that weapon formed against us pierced us, but as Isaiah 54:17 says, did not prosper. My heart was still bleeding weeks later, but I held on to faith and hope. In the midst of severe heart pain and buckets of tears I said to Jesus, "Lord, I'm grieving, but I'm grateful." I knew God would not leave me in that broken place. Indeed, He brought me through it.

God heals more than physical ailments. He heals hurt emotions and broken hearts, too. If you are still hurt after past relationship trauma and drama, God can heal you, too.

It is natural and healthy to grieve a broken relationship. Grieving is beneficial because it helps you purge painful emotions. It allows you to release strong emotions such as shock, sorrow, anger, disappointment, discontent, rejection, embarrassment, shame, lack of understanding and other deep feelings rather than exploding into self-destructive violent, outbursts that may occur when you bottle up more emotions than your heart and mind can handle internally.

Every person does not grieve the same way, but the experience is painful to all. Grieving can be startling at first and its demonstration can cause you to wonder if you are really okay. The excruciating emotional pain resulting from rejection and failure in an unsuccessful relationship can cause even the toughest man to curl up in the fetal position and weep. It can also cause the tender heart of the sweetest woman to become numb and hard as a rock.

Often people try to smoke, sex, eat, spend, drink, medicate or gamble their grief away. You must realize that the power to end your grief cannot be found in rage and retaliation or any kind of harmful binge. Healing can not be found in marijuana, alcohol or any other drug. When these highs wear off, you will come down and find the same bitter realities. Constantly recommitting the same sin to numb the pain of not dealing with reality can lead you to addiction. Your last state will then be worse than the first and you will still be grief stricken. Please, let God help you.

Listen to someone who has survived some deep valleys. Trouble can not and will not last always. Weeping may endure for a night, but God's promise is that joy will come in the morning. Grief's intensity is great at first, but it will lessen with time when you do not resist it, but rather allow yourself to go through its process. If you feel you are not healing well after a relationship that fell apart three months ago or more, you may be feeling that way because you have avoided going through the grief process. The Lord is listening 24 hours each day and 7 days each week, so tell Him all about it. Grab a teddy bear, shed your tears and set those angry emotions free. Writing letters, poetry and journaling are also constructive ways to release grief.

Grief is a very emotional time. It is not meant to last forever, but it is an essential part of your prescription for healing. The grieving period has no specific number of days, weeks, or months; however, it does need to run its course. Many job benefits include bereavement leave when a close loved one physically dies. None I know of offer bereavement leave to mourn the death of your relationship, but you may need to take a few days off to grieve and rest. Do not try to outrun grief because it will catch up with you.

Most people fear what they are not familiar with. Now that you know it's natural, do not fear grief, but accept it as a vital step on your path to total recovery. After grieving sufficiently, you can be healed, restored and begin your life again after break-ups, separation, divorce and even the death of a spouse. Let's walk hand in hand through this valley to help you become whole and able to love again.

Divorce causes grief.

I wish it was the truth that all couples wed with clean hearts and clear minds with hopes and plans for their bond to last forever, but hearing the unspoken motives behind many of today's marriages might surprise you. These days, people make the marriage commitment for traditional and not so traditional reasons. Some women get married only for financial security, because of pressure from and the influence of family and friends, because their biological clock is rapidly ticking, fear of being called an old maid, or the perceived prestige associated with having a man's last name. Some men get married for fear of loneliness, as an ego booster--to look macho in public with a woman on his arm, to fulfill a perceived expectation of a leadership role, for legal sex only or for other various reasons and purposes that may or may not be contrary to God's perfect will.

Most likely, you know someone who got married as revenge--thinking they were punishing or making an ex-lover jealous. Even in the spiritual setting of the church, many have married temporary fixes, not their true mates, to have sex legally and biblically or free themselves from guilt of premarital sexual activity, not because God knitted their hearts together and has a divine purpose for them to walk as one. The size of a wedding does not matter. If a marriage is entered into for the wrong motive, it won't last.

It is a quick and easy process to get married, but it's longer and more painful to end it. The national divorce rate is over 50% and seems to be climbing. Half of the marriages are lasting, but unfortunately, many still end with divorce.

A night club radio advertisement surprised me recently. This unforgettable commercial was promoting a night club's usual schedule of events as well as publicizing that they hosted private parties. As the announcer blurted party suggestions, I was stunned to hear that in addition to anniversaries and birthdays, *divorce* was mentioned as an occasion to have a party there!

It was my first time hearing the divorce party idea publicized so freely. It seemed almost as if the club implied that people should automatically expect it to happen to them. That bothered me, because although the divorce rate seems high, there is still great hope for many marriages to be in the percentage that make it. In fact, I expect mine to be in the even smaller percentage that is fabulously happy, experiencing marriage the way God originally intended.

I was perplexed. Did this nightclub realize they were advertising a party to celebrate death? Divorce is the death of a relationship as it formerly existed. Divorcees must acknowledge that although they may still communicate to discuss children or assets and may even consider each other as friends, it's not the same. It was difficult for me to visualize a party at any location to "celebrate" a couple's divorce. When a spouse narrowly escapes a physically abusive marriage alive, I can imagine him or her privately rejoicing, thanking God for his or her life. But in the case of non-abusive marriages, even a "peaceful" divorce leaves one or both ex-spouses with some negative emotions, hard feelings, deep hurt and regret--feeling like they wasted years of their life and wondering if they will recover them.

Divorce hurts. It is like a violent earthquake that shakes lives and collapses relationships, disturbing and destroying the security of a family expected to stand forever. It sometimes happens unexpectedly and cannot always be prevented. Divorcees may be so blessed to walk away bruised and dusty from the aftermath, but they can also suffer permanent injuries or become emotional casualties.

Tremors can occur after an earthquake. Even when divorcees do not publicly acknowledge it, most experience some type of grief after signing separation agreements and finalizing divorce papers. Since a successful marriage requires a willing wife and husband, the spouse who sacrificed most and gave their all usually hurts the most.

Forced to move on into an unread chapter of their lives, divorcees often need help--prayer, therapy, counseling, support groups, a shoulder to cry on--to overcome their grief. Many were publicly humiliated by the situations that led them to divorce court. Their emotions may still feel the sting of infidelity, arguments and abuse. Some despise the thought of entering the dating scene again and many have mixed emotions about their new marital statuses.

It takes time to get your life back together after divorce. Thus, the real truth--even when people act like they are celebrating a separation or divorce in public, they likely experience some somber moments in private settings. If you are friends with a recent divorcee who talks like he or she is on top of the world, stay close and encourage them anyway. Why? The denial of hurt is often strong evidence that he or she is grief-stricken. But this, too, shall pass.

Am I bitter or better?

I've seen people reject caring, committed lovers and ruin good marriages because they still had open wounds from former relationships. Visualize this. In marriage number one, the husband cheated repeatedly, and this, among other issues, resulted in divorce. The wife remarried, but the fear that her new husband would repeat the mistakes of the last one tormented her daily. Insecure because of her past, she "stalks" her new husband to the point that he is beyond frustration. Weary from her not trusting him, husband number two walks out the door. In this scenario, the wife became distrustful of the wrong man. Still hurting, she could not separate her present husband who genuinely cared for her from the past man who hurt her.

Or imagine that a wife was unfaithful to her husband and they divorced. He was so macho, so the pain, shame and embarrassment were excruciating. He later remarried on the rebound. In carefully strategizing to minimize his risk of being cheated on, he settled for a woman who lessened his loneliness temporarily, but did not fully satisfy him. As God healed his heart and opened his eyes, he found himself yearning for more. Miserable, he realized his manmade marriage hid but didn't heal his emotional pain.

Is it really fair to judge all men or women with the same measuring stick or to cause your present date or mate to suffer because of what the past one did or did not do? No! The above scenarios are not examples of people walking in their healing, but still living in their hurt. It is hard to have a successful new relationship when you are not healed and have not let go and forgiven the person who hurt you.

I hope you now realize how essential it is to take time to grieve broken relationships. Taking time to grieve will also help you prevent future mistakes that can sidetrack you from God's perfect plan for your destiny. It also helps you process your pain so that you can be restored to emotional health. Then, you can become *better* instead of *bitter*.

When you are still hurting, it is very challenging not to become bitter, distant and pessimistic. I must ask you this serious question. When you think about past relationships that went downhill, are you now *bitter* or *better*?

Does it bother you when other couples seem happy? Have you been through so much that you find yourself in unbelief over the possibility of having a relationship that does not end in heartbreak or divorce? When someone announces a marriage, do you automatically think or say they will end in divorce court? Have you ever attempted to sabotage or discredit someone else's happy relationship? Have you ever whispered doubt in someone's ear to get them to question and distrust a trustworthy date or mate?

If you answered "yes" to one or more of those questions, you just tested positive for *bitterness*. The results are confidential. Now that you are officially diagnosed, we can begin targeted treatment to the infected areas. Your heart shows signs of past trauma and your soul, which is where your emotions dwell, has been damaged, too. Continue reading as antibiotics are being injected into your system right now to prevent any further damage. You can recover. From this point forward, you are on your way to healing!

Choose To Forgive. *"I will let go and let God handle them."*

When you read the quote at the beginning of the chapter, what did you immediately think about? Just to refresh you, it said, *"When you are truly tired of the way things are, you will make a change and no longer wait for a change. Be the change you desire."* Well, the change I am suggesting may not be what you first thought. The change you must make that I am referring to is *choosing to forgive*. So let's walk hand in hand as you start your journey to forgiveness.

Before you say you are ready for a dream relationship, I must tell you that forgiveness is the key to its door. To forgive means to fully release the person who offended you to God to let Him handle and pay him or her back. But there is more. When you forgive, you release the person who hurt you *and* your pain to God. Then you trust God to take care of vengeance, for it belongs to Him. Furthermore, God requires us to forgive if we expect His forgiveness.

Choosing to forgive is not always easy to do, but with the Lord's help you can forgive someone completely. Let's keep it real. It is not ever easy to forgive. After you have been wounded, the first temptation is to express your anger and take revenge on that lover to cause his or her heart or body to bleed. Thoughts of inflicting emotional wounds, physical injury or damaging something your significant other holds dear (like scratching his or her car or burning the clothes) bombard you. In the heat of the moment, that temptation is so real, but you must take your hands off and leave vengeance up to God. Then, stop focusing on revenge and focus on getting the healing you so desperately need.

The only way a victim can become a victor is to forgive.

Forgiveness opens the door to your complete healing. Have you forgiven an ex-lover who mishandled you? Have you forgiven yourself for letting go of Mr. Right or for choosing Mrs. Wrong? If you answered "no" to one or both of those questions, more than likely you are still brokenhearted and suffering because of those mistakes. You may have the public fooled by your smile and put-together outward appearance, but you may be living daily with unforgiveness toward someone else or even yourself. God wants to be your healer and the lifter of your head.

Do you still hold any grudges against living or dead persons who offended you? If you do, did you know that the longer you hold on to that hurt, the stronger bitterness' grip gets? It can send you to an early grave. In order to have total, perfect peace again and no more hatred in your heart, forgiveness is not optional. It's an absolute necessity!

When forgiving, you must realize that its purpose is not to change the person who hurt you, but to change *you*. When you choose not to forgive, you do not hurt your offender, but you hurt and hinder yourself. When you hold a grudge, have a cold heart, turn a deaf ear, plot revenge or do any acts connected to unforgiveness, you damage the person in the mirror much more than you think you are hurting your heartbreaker. I don't know its author, but this truthful quote, "Unforgiveness is like you drinking poison and thinking it will kill the other person," impacted me. It makes sense. Think about it. Nobody should be worth you hurting yourself more than they have already hurt you!

To have a victorious future you must forgive the past.

If you want to experience a future that's better than your past, it is *mandatory* to forgive. Forgiveness is the doorway to forsaking bitterness and becoming *better* because ultimately, forgiveness opens the door for your heart to be mended, healed and made whole again.

Matthew 6:14 states that when you forgive people of their trespasses against you, God will forgive you when you need it. The Amplified Bible further describes men's trespasses as "reckless and willful sins" and elaborates that you should "let them go and give up resentment." If you do not forgive others, let them go and give up resentment, you will not be able to find forgiveness when you need it. As long as we are breathing, we will need His forgiveness!

It can seem extremely hard to choose to forgive someone who you feel should apologize to you first. I felt that when God told me I needed to call and release a former "friend" from the hurt she caused me. I asked God, "Why should I have to apologize and release her when I did not hurt her?" "Because," He said. "You forgiving her is not for *her* benefit. You have to do this to get the healing *you* need."

So what should you do when offenders refuse to humble themselves and apologize? Forgive them anyway. If you choose not to, you will remain bitter and give their weapons power to work. Do you realize how much more victory they get if you continue to be angry until they do apologize, which may never happen? Don't remain bound. We cannot always prevent people from hurting us, but we possess the power to receive our healing when we forgive.

Forgiving may not be easy, but it will always be worth it!

Most people get stuck somewhere in between trying to forgive and holding on to a grudge. Greater peace and the ability to move beyond your pain is so much better than the discomfort of carrying resentment's heavy baggage.

Total forgiveness and healing is not always instant. In fact, it can be a lengthy process that sometimes takes days, weeks, months or even years. I have had salt poured in old wounds when I saw people whose loose lips and evil deeds hurt me deeply. I knew I had forgiven and released them to God, but when I became emotional at the remembrance of the situation, I knew God was not finished healing me yet.

The enemy quickly reminded me of what they did to sabotage my relationship, especially when it seemed they were moving on or what their lips tried to stop in my life was happening for them. God reminded me that vengeance belongs to Him. I ran to my secret place, laid prostrate, prayed and cried out to God! I needed more of His healing.

Philippians 4:13, "I can do all things through Christ who strengthens me," enabled me to forgive individuals who it was very hard to forgive. One time God did not allow me to confront my offenders. When I held my peace as they spoke and acted as if they had not done me any harm, I knew more than ever just how real Jesus is! You just don't know how hard that was! I wanted to approach them and make them aware of their offenses, but though they acted spiritual, their deeds proved they were not mature. But, the Lord blessed me to move on as He assured me that He would handle their payback in greater ways than I could.

Forgive those who hurt you, but forgive yourself also.

I hope you are now convinced to forgive others quickly, but also remember to forgive yourself when needed. In order for you not to live a life of regret or remain bound by people who remember the sins you committed, you must forgive yourself, too, and walk in your new beginning.

We are all works in progress. If you are reading this sentence, you have not made it to heaven yet; therefore, God is still perfecting you. You are still dying daily to sin. I pray that you are not stagnant, but increasing in God's love and power, growing from faith to faith and glory to glory.

We have all made some type of mistakes. As I like to say, noone has dotted every 'I' and crossed every 'T'. Let's be honest. Even if you have been morally upright and have not sinned openly, you have sinned secretly before. Secret sins include matters of the heart that need to be addressed that God sees, but man cannot see on the surface.

Those who have stopped sinning outwardly have missed His mark, too. I have often met and fellowshipped with people who seem to have public sins in order, but Holy Spirit knows every private, inner issue they have that is not pleasing to God. For example, some "Christians" have not surrendered their itching ear for gossip to the Lord and are guilty of having an uncontrolled tongue that secretly tears people down rather than build them up. Yes, God sees manipulation, gossip, being two-faced and being a busybody in other's affairs as sins, too. Whatever secret sins you are dealing with, repent, submit yourself and those sins to the Lord. There is nothing hidden from Him.

Romans 3:23 states that we all have sinned and come short of the glory of God. Isaiah 64:6 declares that all of your righteousnesses, your good deeds, are as filthy rags. Even when you think you are walking upright, you need to watch out and not forget that you walk in a flesh suit daily.

But perhaps you did sin openly. You may have abused alcohol and other drugs, had an abortion or children out of wedlock, had an extramarital affair, was involved in prostitution or pornography, dealt drugs, were a liar or murderer, homosexual or were rightfully incarcerated. Some of us have done things that certain people refuse to let us forget. Remember, they do not have a heaven or hell to put you in. Not one of those sins is unforgivable by God.

Your future does not have to be ruined by a past mistake you made. God is a forgiving God who is able and willing to forgive you, even when you do not deserve it. He is not pleased with your behaviors that are not like Him, nor does He expect you to continue in confessed sin, but Jesus has already died that you and I could be forgiven. Hallelujah! God forgives you when you confess your sins and repent!

If God can forgive you, you can forgive yourself. He knows your past, but He also sees your brighter future. Some of the people God used in the Bible had terrible pasts that included lying, adultery and even murder! But, when they surrendered to God, He changed their futures. In fact, we now read the testimonies and triumphs of David--once caught in adultery, Saul--once a shameless persecutor of Christians, Moses--once a murderer and others. When you confess your sins to God, He forgives and forgets!

Give God your desire to get even.

Have you ever taken matters into your own hands? Have you ever felt like giving someone a black eye, a thorough fussing or cussing out, breaking a few bones or hitting him or her where it hurts physically and emotionally would be satisfying and just punishment for his or her wrong done toward you? One verse you need to remember in times like these is Romans 12:19, "Vengeance is mine. I shall repay." It reminds us to let go and let God.

You can get yourself in trouble conspiring evil plots against others. II Corinthians 2:4 tells Christians that the weapons of your warfare are NOT carnal, but mighty through God to the pulling down of strongholds. Stop trying to fight back with an unruly tongue and devilish deeds. You will only win when you let God fight for you.

You need to know that God does not like it when people do you wrong for no reason. When you have been victimized by someone demonstrating one or more of the evil behaviors the Lord absolutely hates in Proverbs 6:16-19, God will fight for you. You don't have to worry about getback or revenge. He will handle it better than you can.

You may be thinking, how can God be good and get vengeance on my enemies? God is patient, loving and kind, but He is also a God of justice. He loves to see justice executed for wrong done to those in rightstanding with Him. Like a loving natural parent, God will discipline you when you are wrong, but He will defend you when you are right. He can get fierce when His babies have been hurt by the evil deeds of another. Don't play with my Daddy!

Forgive and free yourself.

Though forgiveness enables you to love purely, it does not always lead to the reinstatement of relationships. When offering forgiveness, do not let a person who has not repented make you feel obligated to accept them back in your life to the same place they were before they hurt you.

Ignorance of the fact that an unrepentant person may hurt you again is not bliss. Since the Bible encourages you to be wise as a serpent and harmless as a dove, *it is okay* to love forgiven people with consistent negative behaviors from a distance. If they continue to repeat the same actions that caused you pain, you must decide whether or not it is healthy for you to expose yourself again to their behaviors and attitudes. Like my daddy taught me, if the dog bites you once, it is the dog's fault. If he bites you twice, it is yours. Mama did not raise any fools either. Unpack your bags and do not let anyone take you on a guilt trip when you choose not to allow their drama back in your life.

People quickly forget that consequences arise when they act unseemly toward others. Some have gotten away with their mistreatment and abuse for so long that they think their victims will remain naïve to their manipulations. Just in case you are the offender, you need to accept that persons you have caused emotional pain may truly forgive you, but they may not want you back in their lives. You cannot force them to love you. Your presence may be a reminder of past pain or they may not be able to trust you. As II Corinthians 7:10 says, repent and be godly sorry. Change, so you can be ready for your future chance at love.

Let go and let God.

If you want to have *love without the drama*, you must let go of bitterness, anger and resentment and forgive, forgive, forgive. Your flesh resists letting offenses go and putting your plans for revenge in God's hands, but with God's help you can definitely do it. When you surrender your desire for revenge to Him and forgive those who hurt and offended you, He will take the sting out of your past pain.

In relationships, some offenses seem harder to forgive and let go of than others. Even after excruciating emotional pain, I learned that I had to forgive in order to free myself from misery, hurt and suffering that would linger if I chose not to forgive and let go. Reading in His Holy Bible that God required me to forgive if I expected His forgiveness for my mess-ups convinced me to forgive even when it was difficult. It also kept me from taking matters into my own hands. The enemy's torment on an emotionally stressful day can make you feel that launching hurtful arrows at the person who hurt you or another easy target is a justifiable release of your anger. But that is not the proper way. If you take revenge in your own hands, not only will God repay the person who hurt you, but He will discipline you, too.

It may be your flesh's first reaction, but it is not like Christ to desire to or make others hurt as much as or more than you have. It is the enemy of your soul that influences you to reenact toward any persons--unsuspecting dates or mates, friends or family in happy relationships, coworkers, the public and even your enemies--the actions that have traumatized you. You do not have to act on evil thoughts.

Once I learned that hurting people hurt other innocent people, I could love and not hate the people who hurt me. God empowered me to pray for their emotional healing so that they, too, would be delivered from drama. Isn't that amazing? That's when I knew God had saved me for real!

Let's see if you can pass the unconditional love test. If your enemy's car was stranded on the roadside and you could help, would you drive by and say, "Good enough for you," or would you assist them? If you can stop to help, that is loving them with the love of God. Proverbs 25:22 says you will heap coals of fire on their heads. It takes a big person to bless an enemy. Are you becoming better yet?

God loves us and wishes that noone should perish. It sounds hard and often seems unfair to love our enemies, but it pleases God to love them as one of His children. However, you don't have to be best friends or lovers again. Some situations require you to love people from a distance.

Some person's character cannot be trusted, as my grandmother used to say, any farther than you can throw an elephant. All who apologize may not be worthy of being back in your inner circle. Pray about it. Unless they have truly repented to God and you and matured, it's hard to be sure they will not hurt, betray or deceive you again. It is unwise to closely reassociate with people with unchanged hearts and minds. Why set yourself up for another setback?

Satan is crafty. Some "sweet nothings" in your ear are just that, nothing! Matthew 10:16 admonishes us to be wise as serpents and harmless as doves. II Corinthians 11:14 says Satan masquerades as an angel of light. Don't fall for the okeydoke or guilt trips, which are setups for persons to slither like a serpent back into your life. When you are sure you have forgiven, do not let anyone manipulate you into accepting them or another offender back to the same role they previously played in your life, okay? Remember that. Now let's review ten facts about forgiveness.

1. God forgives us and He expects us to forgive.
2. Forgiveness is a straight choice; you choose to do it wholeheartedly or you choose not to forgive at all.
3. The "amount" of forgiveness you offer is not to be based on the type of wrong someone else has done.
4. When you forgive, God can help you forget.
5. Forgiveness is not for the other person. It's for you.
6. Forgive others, but don't neglect to forgive yourself.
7. Vengeance belongs to God, so let Him fight for you.
8. You must forgive the past to have a victorious future.
9. True forgiveness opens the door to your healing.
10. Victims become victors when they finally forgive.

You do not have to remain bitter. God wants to heal you and make you better! When you forgive and release the desire to get even, your enemies will not be able to hold you down any longer. Plus, you can have clean hands and a clean heart because God will handle revenge for you. So let go of that bitterness, anger and resentment. Choose to forgive the people who hurt you, and let God, Who loves you more than you can imagine, heal you from heartbreak!

I Am Hurting And I Want To Be Healed.

Hurting people hurt other people. If you are not healed, you will repeat the hurts others inflicted upon you. When you enter into a new relationship before you are healed from past hurt, your new love can become an innocent victim, penalized for the wrongs of your past date or mate.

When hurt is in your heart, the enemy continually suggests revenge! He definitely directs you to avenge the person who hurt you. Even worse, he plants thoughts in your mind to hurt and cause broken-heartedness in people who were not even involved in your relationship's failure.

Some angry, unhealed persons spend an incredible amount of energy envying and attempting to sabotage other happy people. As I so painfully learned after an assassination attempt on my joyful friendship-relationship, everybody is not happy for you. Your radiant love glow illuminates the world around you, yet your shining light can expose another person's hidden misery. When those persons are your family or close friends, the painful shock stabs your heart like a murderer with a machete. Thank God for being a healer. His supernatural surgery can stop your heart from bleeding and jumpstart it to beat again.

When you face disappointment, rejection, betrayal, separation, divorce and any other hurt, you must allow yourself time to grieve so that the healing process can begin. When people leap into new relationships before grieving, forgiving and healing from past hurts, the new one almost always ends in misery and heartbreak. Here are tried and tested tips to help you heal from your heartbreak.

Hints To Help You Heal From Heartbreak

1. **Grieve.** It's normal to cry. Even the strongest of hearts bleed. Relieve yourself of feeling the need to impress family, friends or community by trying to act like you were not hurt by your break-up, failed marriage or bad choice. Weeping may endure for a night, but joy will return.

2. **Develop platonic friendships with the opposite sex.** Having healthy, non-sexual interactions with them will help rebuild your confidence in the good qualities of men or women. This may be challenging, but it can be done.

3. **Choose a positive outlook and expect brighter days.** View your past as a vehicle's rear view mirror and your future as the windshield. You will wreck looking back while driving, so glance at life's rear view mirror briefly.

4. **Forgive, for you will need to be forgiven one day.**

5. **Talk to someone who can help you.** Seek and speak to positive, uplifting people. Avoid judgmental critics. Stop complaining and cancel all invitations to your pity party.

6. **Take time to get refreshed in the presence of the Lord.** Go to church and Christian events often. Pray. Read the Bible daily. Join a life group or other spiritual fellowship.

7. **Get involved in life. Participate in positive activities.** Attend motivational seminars that help you refocus your energy on positive things. Join a network or volunteer.

My friend, your healing from every heartbreak can be found at the feet of Jesus when you finally totally forgive yourself, those who you were in relationship with and those whose words and actions contributed to the oversight, sabotage or failure of a treasured relationship. If you believe healing can only come after you wait for others to apologize to you and ask for your forgiveness, you may be waiting for it a long time. Pride prevents countless people from confessing to their wrongdoings, so that may never happen. Do you plan to stay broken until it does?

Thank God, your healing from heartbreak does not depend upon another's apology; however, it is contingent on your willingness to forgive. With God's help you can do it. So why don't you choose to forgive, let go of the hurt, pain and shame and let God handle all revenge.

Isn't it comforting to know you can receive the heart healing you need when you forgive and let go? You no longer have any reason to keep holding on to negativity and heartache. Harboring resentment does not benefit you. Let go of envy, anger and the heartbreaks that have held you back. You now know that with God it is possible to forgive people for any and everything they have done to you because forgiveness is not up to them, it's up to you.

Loving life and letting go of your past is beneficial to your health and lifestyle. Now that you know that you do not need that lover or friend's apology before you can be healed from past hurt, you can start your journey to being healed from heartbreak. God wants you to be restored after broken relationships. Beloved, forgiveness starts with you.

God does work in mysterious ways. You may have to do what I did to become free from hurt caused by the actions of others. The Lord unctioned *me* to be the first one to make a phone call and offer forgiveness to someone who blatantly hurt me but had never apologized. I hesitated, but my spirit knew it was the only solution to relieve my inner pain. When I called, a weight was lifted. It felt so good that the next day, I called a few more people I did no wrong to and asked their forgiveness just to clear the air. Most were amazed that I humbled myself in that way. They did not apologize to me, but regardless of their responses, my mission was accomplished. I had a clean heart and hands.

It is a wonderful feeling when you are free and finally on top of the unforgiveness and bitterness that used to hold you down. I benefited the most by offering forgiveness. Like me, you will know when you have totally forgiven and received God's complete healing when you no longer feel pain associated with the names, faces and any reminders of the persons who hurt you. Are you ready to be free? Why don't you forgive those who hurt you so you, too, can experience the great peace and joy God gave me?

Forgiveness may not always be easy, but it will always be worth it. Its benefits far outweigh the costs of the heavy toll of trying to carry a grudge to your grave. Like me, you may feel a weight lift off your chest and your broken heart will heal when you forgive. Your attitude may become more positive and your physical health may improve, too. The Lord is waiting for you to ask Him to help you do what previously has been hard to do on your own--forgive!

Are you still bitter or are you better?

Are you still stubbornly holding on to a grudge? You do not have to aim to get even or plot revenge on those who have hurt you any longer. Aim to get over the hurt, pain and shame that you have carried around much too long.

Perhaps you do not totally like the person you have become over the years. If you have purposefully wronged others in the past, some bad things may be happening to you right now because you are reaping the fruit of the evil deeds you have sown. Perhaps now you realize how terrible the people you hurt must have felt when you betrayed their trust with your infidelity, gossip, lies, discord or deception. Reaping the multiplied harvest of bad seeds you sowed and wrongs you committed against others is another good reason to stop acting out of misery and bitterness and turn over a new leaf to become better.

On the contrary, you may not have chosen to experience the heartaches you've felt. Rape, molestation or abuse may have left you feeling stripped of virtue and self-esteem. Divorce may have left you feeling stripped of your pride and family dreams. Lies and persecution may have left you feeling stripped of your integrity. But even in the midst of every unfair crime, you were not stripped of one thing. Nothing can strip you of the power to choose to forgive!

Now that you know just how forgiving God is, you can forgive yourself and extend His abundant forgiveness to others. The great news is that you don't have to remain miserable and bitter. You can be healed from heartbreak. Yes, you can become better when you choose to forgive!

ACT 2

Defining The Dream

CHAPTER FOUR

Three Things Every Woman Wants

The drama-free man is motivated to know his woman's dreams.
- Lynetta Jordan

A man of excellence who aims to please should treasure his woman enough to help her realize personal ambitions and relationship dreams. Although sex is a top priority for most men, it is erroneous to think that exploring what women want is limited to a discussion of how to satisfy them sexually. Married women should enjoy the romantic romp, but to be fulfilled, wives need more than thrilling lovemaking that makes them call their husbands "daddy!" I would never underestimate the tremendous impact of sexual fulfillment on overall marital satisfaction; however, heterosexual women of all ages, nationalities, shapes, and sizes also desire strong heterosexual men who will treat them like cherished queens and bring out the best in them.

Most men secretly fear failure and rejection. Every man appreciates his woman's clear communication of what she wants for holiday, birthday and anniversary gifts so he can be sure he pleases her. So men, write this down and put it in your wallets. Every woman wants the man who holds her hand and heart to *lead* her, *listen* to her and *love* her.

Every Woman Wants Her Man To Lead Her.

In the old television show *Leave It To Beaver*, it was easy to see the husband providing for his household while the wife remained at home cooking, cleaning and raising their children. That show was in black in white, but it provided an unmistakably clear picture of a responsible man taking pleasure in making daily efforts to provide for his family.

Society has changed since the days of *Leave It To Beaver*. Television is now broadcast in brilliant color. In contrast, many modern day women work outside their homes and send their children to daycare. Some are fortunate enough to hire someone else to cook and clean for them. But no matter how independent, educated, or spiritual a woman may be, she still needs her man to be a strong provider and lead her to higher heights than she can venture alone.

God initially established man's leadership position in Genesis, the first book of the Bible, when He gave Adam the responsibility of naming the living creatures and tending the garden of Eden. That was his job, his duty, his assignment. God gave Adam his wife after his job, that is, after He established him in his own authority and role.

God is also counting on today's men to stand up and lead their households in serving the Lord. Adam was the first man to have God-given responsibility to lead his family and encourage them to honor God wholeheartedly. Suffering occurred when He did not follow God's specific instructions to the letter and partook of the deceiving fruit with his wife. Men after Adam still suffer when they do not offer godly leadership to their families, too.

Every man needs to have a spiritual *and* natural vision for himself and his household. Proverbs 29:18 states that, "Where there is no vision, the people perish." When a man has no vision, he has no goals with action plans for his own or his family's future. One of the things that makes a male a man is when he walks out the goals he talks about. He implements his action plans and persistently makes active steps of progress toward achieving those goals. Some men talk a good game, but anybody can do that. You must closely watch their lives and see how they follow through.

Some men wander aimlessly about life with a "whatever happens, happens" attitude, taking things as they come, and then are surprised that few doors of opportunity are opening for them. Men with little or no vision can easily find themselves caught in the shameful yoke of bondage of negative addictions like gambling, alcohol or drug abuse. Lack of vision is a trap. This is not how you lead a family.

Spiritual men also need strong natural vision to ensure a balanced lifestyle. Most men without natural vision will have no savings or investments, no health, disability and life insurance policies and no will to provide for future support of their families after death. Men of vision care, plan and prepare to ensure their family's future well-being.

Men who lack natural vision may rely on their mamas, girlfriends or wives to provide for them. Thinking only of themselves, a few of those men may not even feel the need to pursue higher education, a full-time job or career to build a better future for their families and significantly contribute to the household. That is drama with a capital D.

Supportive women understand that men of vision may experience short periods of testing and trial. Most uplift and uphold their men during these seasons, because like winter, spring, summer, and fall, they do not expect those seasons to remain, but change. Job layoffs can cause household finances to decrease for a short time. Physical health issues can emerge and trigger short term disabilities. Grief can paralyze emotions and temporarily limit a man's ability to provide emotional support to others. A woman can respect a strong man who diligently tries in spite of the obstacles on his journey; nevertheless, she may have little or no tolerance for a man who does not demonstrate effort.

Men, if you have not been an example of godly spiritual and natural leadership in your home, now is the time to change the course of your family's future. Do not delay any longer. Confess and repent of your past shortcomings and immediately start changing and lead your family into a brighter, more stable future. Her happiness depends on it.

Before a woman's lips utter dissatisfaction about her man's lack of leadership, she has already felt it in her heart. Even if she has dealt with it quietly for a while, when she starts calculating her contributions to the relationship and carefully analyzes how his lack of leadership is deducting from her overall satisfaction, she may be ready to call it quits. Even in times of intense hardship, it may irritate an optimistic working woman to hear her head of household blame everyone else for his despair. She may be quiet first, but internal combustion can lead to verbal outbursts or emotional explosions. When she just cannot take any more, she may suddenly walk out of the relationship. Men, please pay attention. A woman needs her man to lead her with a clear vision and strong provision for the family's future.

In addition to vision and provision, wives of today need their men to lead in prayer and protection. The man is considered a covering for his wife and children, ensuring that their spiritual, natural and emotional needs are met. He also physically protects them from hurt, harm and danger. As God's appointed priest, the drama-free husband leads his family into spirit-filled worship, prayer and speaks godly and practical wisdom into his family.

A man can only offer his family life-changing heavenly instruction when he is personally connected to God. The drama-free man realizes he must be more than religious. He is more than a church member, leader or officer. This spiritual man is a true worshipper who has a personal prayer life and genuine love relationship with Jesus. This mighty man of valor truly loves the Lord and His people. A true servant of the most high God, He chooses to do what pleases God even when it discomforts his own flesh. A godly man is the best kind of man to be.

Every woman wants the man she loves to lead her into a future that is brighter than her past. In the drama-free marriage, the wife can safely rest and relax in her husband's strong arms of love. His leadership assures her of his love, so she finds it easy to love him since she knows he has her best interests at heart. As he leads with vision, provision, protection and prayer, submitting to the love of her life becomes a joy for the drama-free woman to do.

Every Woman Wants Her Man To Listen To Her.

I recall a listening skills lesson I taught my college Public Speaking class in which I compared hearing and listening. Contrary to most of their beliefs, they are not equivalent.

So what is the difference between hearing and listening? *Hearing* is an automatic, involuntary auditory response. If your ears work, you can hear. You don't choose what you hear because your ears pick up all nearby sounds. But *listening* is selective. It is a voluntary action that requires the listener to focus and pay close attention to a speaker. When someone listens, related responses follow. We have all spoken to people who pretended to listen, but were only hearing because words went in one ear and out the other.

Being listened to makes women feel valued, intelligent and important. A man should listen and respond to his woman's words and heart. Ask about her day and then conversate about it to show it's not just a routine question, but you are listening to her. When she mentions an item she likes, you can try to surprise her with it. Paying attention and complimenting her on positive changes she makes also assures her that you not only hear, but listen to her. A woman who feels listened to is much more likely to be highly attentive to and prioritize her man's every need.

Every husband needs to acknowledge the godly wisdom of his God-ordained wife, his helpmate. Though God made him the top decision-maker, he should realize that listening to God's wisdom flowing through her will benefit the entire family. The Proverbs 31 wife was a wise woman. So men, listen to godly women and show them great love.

Every Woman Wants Her Man To Love Her.

Every woman craves the attention and affection of the man she is dating or married to. Even more than she desires to hear him say those three words, "I love you," she needs him to demonstrate it daily in big and small ways. Small love trinkets can make a big impact on her heart!

A man is God's earthly representative to love a woman. What an amazing feeling and day it was when I told my dream date that I actually felt God loving me through him. I was in awe of God's gift to my life. The overflow of spiritual and natural love I felt from him was undeniable. I prayed every step of the way and about every aspect of our friendship since his first call. The more we conversated, the closer we grew. God revealed how our hearts for Him and for one another were on one accord. We even had the same favorite worship song, performed by different artists. This was love on God's level like I had not experienced before!

Loving his lady abundantly can help a man's woman love him better if it is in her heart to love him. Ephesians 5:36 commands husbands to love their wives as Christ loves the church. The love God has for His church is active and forgiving. The book of Hosea tells a symbolic story of Christ's everlasting love for His bride, the church, who has betrayed its first love (God) and ran after other lovers (false religions). God commanded Hosea to marry a prostitute and then do what many husbands of today will not, pursue and continue to love her after she betrayed him. God used Hosea to demonstrate that He is always wooing the church with His passionate, unconditional and enduring love!

I John 4:18 states that "perfect love casts out fear." Men, leading, listening to and loving your woman helps her feel secure and calms any fear that she will not be provided for, protected and loved by you. Loving a woman perfectly is motivation to cast out the fear of failure. I recall the phrase, "Nothing beats a failure but a try." Don't be so afraid of failing that you play the blame game and make excuses to avoid being a better provider. When you risk losing your family by not making life better for them, you have already failed. II Timothy 2:15 explains that the spirit of fear is not from God, so fight that fear that's trying to hold you back!

Loving anyone with Christ-like love is a tall order that only a heart connected to Jesus can fill. I encourage you to read I Corinthians 13's list of the attributes of true love. Love is patient, kind and forgiving. I love verse 8, "Love never fails," the best. *Lust* and any other alternate motive will fail, but as Song of Solomon 8:7 says, "Many waters cannot quench *love*. Neither can floods drown it."

God made love a powerful force. Loving her perfectly can be a tough job, but it is what every woman wants. Your consistent demonstration of faithfulness, commitment and responsibility can help ease any external fears she may have of your love for her being short-lived or inconsistent.

If you are a man who does not have clearly defined goals, it's time to write your vision for your relationship. Love God first and make your woman heart's your target. Building better relationships require efforts from both of you. Do your part to hit the bullseye when you aim directly at her heart by leading her, listening to her and loving her.

CHAPTER FIVE

Three Things Every Man Needs

A drama-free woman is sensitive and attentive to her man's needs.
- Lynetta Jordan

To have *love without the drama*, a woman cannot leave all relationship maintenance up to her beau or husband. A drama-free must woman recognize that she is a significant contributor to her relationship's success. She should be as concerned about improving it as she expects her man to be, so she should give love abundantly and endeavor to show as much attention and affection as she expects to receive. As she does, she will reap the benefits of loving God's man!

As Proverbs 14:1 says, "A wise woman builds her house, but a foolish one plucks it down with her own hands." That scripture makes it clear that a woman plays a major role in nurturing her successful intimate relationship. A married woman must create a home her husband is happy to return to. If you are single, prepare now for a future happy home.

Love thrives when relationships are mutually beneficial to both the man and woman. Since I have addressed what women want, I would not dare minimize the significance of what men need. The Lord revealed that every man needs his woman to *pose for him, play with him* and *praise him*.

These three things that every man needs from his woman are "hot off the Holy Ghost press!" That's Lynetta's slang that means that it's a God-given revelation, not my own. As a college educated woman with an earned master's degree, I respect research and education. But let me tell you, I respect God's voice even more. With scripture, He clearly confirmed each one of the three needs He spoke to me.

Before I delve deeper, let me emphasize the importance of a woman contributing to relationship success. A woman should aim to create unforgettable experiences for the man she adores. It's not always what you do, but it's how you do it. For example, I have been complimented on making a simple meal romantic and unforgettable by serving it with sparkling grape juice in gold-trimmed champagne glasses. This elegant touch showed that I valued and honored him so much that I served him with the best. He deserved it. Men forever remember when women pour on exclusive and extravagant love. So wise women, build your houses!

Recently, an afternoon conversation with a married couple led to a casual counseling session right in their living room! They were as close as two peas in a pod, yet I perceived that both of them had unspoken desires and unmet needs. As God ministered to them through me, I shared what every woman wants and every man needs with them as I tried to help bridge their gender gaps. Men and women are "wired" differently, but God uniquely designed us to complement, not contradict each other. Our differences are not designed to separate us, but to complete us as two persons unite to become a more powerful team.

As we continued to talk, Holy Spirit led me to help them discover just how much their past relationship role models and mentors impacted their present perspectives in their own marriage. When you are striving to be the best mate you can, it can be frustrating or joyful to examine your upbringing, but you must face it. They soon realized how much what they witnessed and believed about love, life and relationships in their youth influenced them as adults.

For most people, it is easiest to treat a mate like you saw your parental figures treating each other in marriage or love relationships. Some very fortunate individuals grew up with great role models who were married and affectionate and demonstrated a healthy, non-abusive, Christ-centered relationship. But you and I know that was not 100% of households. It may not have even been a good 75% that were truly happy. All persons did not see romantic love displayed by couples who claimed to "love" each other. The remainder saw the exact opposite--verbally or physically abusive, emotionally disconnected parents who lived under the same roof, but sometimes in separate bedrooms. Some saw miserable couples who lived inside the house but gave their love outside the home. Some were not married at all. So how do you think they define love?

Couples need to understand how each other wants and needs to be loved. As I continued to minister to this couple, their eyes opened when I connected their past experiences to their present expectations. Before I left, I shared practical examples to help ensure understanding and satisfaction of each other's emotional needs. I believe they acted on them!

If you did not grow up with positive models of nourishing, mutually beneficial relationships, that is no longer an excuse to let your love lack or fail. Too many resources are available to help you learn to love better. You can tear your house down with your own hands when you are always bickering, fussy and complaining. Proverbs 21:19 says a man would rather dwell in the wilderness than with a contentious woman. Be easy to communicate with and attentive to his needs. You do not want to leave voids for another to fill. By the way, please note that if you are unmarried, it's not your role to meet his physical needs yet!

As Titus 2 instructs, the older women should teach the younger. Older is not just age, but maturity and wisdom, so let me encourage you. Ladies, if past hurt has you afraid to love again, let me say this. Sharing your heart in a healthy relationship with a compatible man whose life is not only Christ-centered, but *surrendered* to Christ will bring healthy harvests of love. When you assess your relationship, your emotions can account for his positive net worth. One character trait of this "good" man is that he has pure motives and is not a deceiver. At first, his arrival in your life may seem too good to be true, but his value, like a maturing investment, will always increase over time. This drama-free man genuinely cares about what his lady wants, needs and desires. A godly man's lady should make it her business to celebrate, respect and encourage him, too. If he is as wonderful as you tell your friends that he is, release your fear from past failures and invest in showing this deserving man love, too.

Pose. *He needs his woman to look um-um good for him.*

What does your hair, dress and smile look like when your date picks you up or your husband comes home? Do you take time to look incredibly lovely and smell extremely good when you go out together? Are you modern and fashionable or dress like you are ten years older? In case you think or feel your appearance no longer matters, let me assure you. He is eyeing you from head to toe babygirl. Even if your man does not say much or compliment you enough, I guarantee he is observing every detail about you.

So what do you really look like for your man? Do you dress in mismatched items when you are in the house or greet him at the door in hair rollers? If so, change that. Even a married woman should step up her appearance a notch. I know a lot of women do not think like that. Some rationalize, "He married me so he loves me just like I am." That may be true that he loves you Plain Jane, but a man is still turned on by sight. Many men are bombarded by billboards of fun, sexy women with beautiful hair and gorgeous smiles on their way home from work. Aim to make his eyes bulge and tongue drop when he sees you!

Knowing that "dressing the part" pleases and delights the man who has chosen you is reason enough for you to make every effort to keep up or step up your personal appearance. It should motivate you to serve him by having good hygiene and attention-getting outward presentation. I believe that every woman should have a personal standard of excellence, so I strive to care for myself well. You should be the first person to take good care of *you*, too.

The way you care for yourself shows a man how to handle you. Single ladies especially, do not wait for a man to come around before you start caring for yourself. Always remember that you must love yourself first before you can love anyone else the right way. Treat yourself to quality dining, make fitness part of your lifestyle, plan spiritual retreats and getaway vacations now. When you take better care of yourself, you will be a lot less likely to let a man abuse, mistreat you or break your spirit.

I do all I personally can to present a positive public and professional image, with or without a man's hand in mine, because I love God and He has taught me to love myself. I recognize that everything I do and the way I do those things speaks volumes about me. My hair, clothes, teeth, and skin matter to me, so I take care of them without anyone telling me to do so. Ladies, are you listening?

When a woman knows a man is paying extra attention, it won't hurt her to do a little extra to enhance herself. For example, I love natural nails, so I keep mine clean and neat. But I have polished my fingernails and toenails in fuschia or bright red to coordinate them with an outfit or had them designed just because I knew a special man had his eyes on me. Although I did it for his enjoyment more than mine, it made me feel even prettier. The more creative I was, the more compliments I received. I loved that he noticed and enjoyed the sound of his sweet praises. I excited him with my unpredictability. That also helped keep his eyes on me.

In biblical times, men delighted in having attractive wives, too. Genesis 24:67 records that when Isaac saw his wife Rebekah for the first time, it was love at first sight. Genesis 29 tells of their son Jacob meeting beautiful Rachel. In verse 11, he kissed her and it made him cry! Rachel was so breathtaking that Jacob worked seven years to marry her. After her father fooled him with her sister Leah, Jacob worked another seven years--a total of 14--to have Rachel as his wife. Rachel must have been a ba-a-a-d sister!

Have you read the description of Proverbs 31's virtuous woman? Her whole life was attractive. An entrepreneur, she was industrious and organized. She lavished abundant love on her family, and in response, they praised her and considered her a woman who excelled among women. In addition, her exceptional efforts caused the men in the city gates to admire her husband. This extraordinary woman's life and deeds made her look extremely attractive to her husband, plus enhanced his public image. The virtuous woman's "posing" made her husband's ratings soar!

It was equally important in Bible times for a lovely woman to pose for her husband at public events, too. It was like a star in a husband's crown for him to have a wife that other men admired--from a distance of course. In the first chapter of the Old Testament book of Esther, King Ahaseurus wanted his wife, Queen Vashti, to pose for him. I believe He wanted his royal court and guests to see how the Lord had favored him with a beautiful wife, not exploit or put her in danger of other men touching her as some suggest. He summoned her to come to his royal feast so he could showcase her beauty. Then a royal no-no happened. Queen Vashti stubbornly refused to come at his request.

Vashti decided that she was not honoring the king's request and refused to appear at dinner that night. It was a disrespectful and rebellious act for the queen not to come when the king summoned her. After that controversial episode, their royal reality show was cancelled. Vashti's decision not to pose publicly for her king disqualified her. She lost her royal status and position as his wife and queen.

Queen Vashti's blatant disrespect resulted in divorce. However, the king's reign and life continued. Vashti was soon replaced by a new queen, Esther, a strong, beautiful handmaiden who was cognizant of the king's rules and was chosen by God "for such a time as this." Consider the consequences ladies. Refusal to pose can disqualify you.

Lastly, husbands need wives to pose in the bedroom. Why should a godly man think about looking at strange flesh in videos, magazines or online when his bride looks delicious? All men with high libidos aren't struggling with lust or sex addiction. They love to make love to their wives!

You should want to be your hubby's exclusive lover and attention getter, so become his personal playgirl! Men are turned on by what they see, so look super sexy. Wear lingerie for him and don't feel like you look like a hooker. As long as he's hooked on you, that's what matters. Pose for personal pictures. Fantasize in your bedroom. Make your house a playland and bring out the boy in your man. Make your superman drive faster than a speeding bullet and leap over tall buildings in a single bound to get home to you! I can't speak for other ladies, but I want to be my husband's one and only playboy bunny. Hop! Hop! Hop!

Play. *He needs his woman to be his best friend and playmate.*

Ladies, that grown man that you are in relationship with needs you to play (<u>P</u>articipate, <u>L</u>augh, <u>A</u>ct <u>Y</u>oung) with him. Life is tough for real men. They proudly provide for their families by going to competitive, demanding jobs where they are often paid less than their true worth and have to outperform other employees. Some daring men own, sustain and manage their own businesses. Since they have to stick their chests out, act tough and show very little emotion in the world of work, they need to be safe to get rid of that façade when they come home to their castles.

I once asked a male friend, my "big" brother, why a love interest was acting in ways that reminded me of a little boy. He was not childish because he was irresponsible. I admired his achievements, responsibility and maturity for his age. But, his behavior was strange and I thought his actions were odd for a man head over heels in love. Like boys can be, he seemed stubborn and in denial. A macho man, he usually acted tough and like he had everything under his control. But now he seemed so scared outside of his comfort zone, just like a lost little boy. My brother's answer calmed and amazed me. He explained gently, "Because inside of every grown man there is a boy."

A man is a grown-up boy. Grown men will occasionally play hide and seek, a game most boys love, with women who make their hearts flutter. Many vulnerable men put up walls and are afraid the objects of their affection will think they are not strong. So they hide and secretly hope you will seek and find them ladies, because that assures them of your love and that they will not fail or be rejected by you. I know that may sound strange because it is contrary to what many men portray, but God knows that the heart of even the toughest, most muscular man is very tender. Like a boy who appreciates his mother's love, a grown man needs and appreciates a woman's warm caress and assuring words when he faces difficult times, too.

No matter what age, everyone looks forward to hanging out and "playing" with their friends. Going out to dinner, sharing a sports activity and watching a favorite movie at home or the theater are all ways for couples to play; however, some couples rarely enjoy outings together.

Unfortunately, all couples do not share a genuine bond of friendship. Every match was not made in heaven. Some feel like they were tricked into marriage, are now trapped in its misery and are trying hard to make the best of a marital mistake which is now a total mishap because they were not put together by God. Others drifted apart over the years as mates pursued separate, individual endeavors. Even more couples had premarital sex too soon and stopped building friendship. As they began focusing on pleasing flesh, long conversations about life, the building blocks to long-term friendship, were replaced by foreplay.

You will enjoy each other more when you are not only sexual partners, but truly friends. Friends know your deep down dirty truths and still love you for real. When you are true friends, there is noone else either of you would rather spend most of your time with. So are the two of you truly friends on the deepest level? Do you know your man "inside and out" like Einstein knew physics ladies? Do you know his ways and deepest thoughts or does a past date or mate know and understand him better? Are you the one he wants to be with or the one he feels situations forced him to be with? Are you together mainly to fulfill sexual needs respectfully or as an outward appearance to satisfy societal or family expectations? Whoa. Tough questions, but your heart knows each answer. Are you really best friends?

One thing true friends do is willingly make sacrifices for each other. That means that they don't complain, keep records or punish the other person later. It's not always pleasant to consider whether or not you have been selfish, but ladies, it is possible your relationship has been more about him meeting your wants than you meeting his needs.

Ladies, what have you sacrificed lately to be your man's playmate? Playing with him includes your joyful participation in recreational activities he enjoys. That says to him that he is important enough for you to reserve special time for him. Whether you spectate or participate, it can be playing in his eyes; however, going just to see if any other women are checking him out does not count. The sole purpose of playing is to spend quality time with him. You can go fishing, play games like tennis, pool or ping pong together or even watch a sport like boxing, basketball or football with him. He knows you may not be a big football fan, but going to a game with him will speak volumes about how much you love and will sacrifice for him. Even if you don't know what a first down is, your presence can make a touchdown in his heart. Now isn't that worth it?

Wives, husbands need you to prioritize sexual play.

If your man wants to be with buddies or work associates more than you, that's a sign that you need to reassess your relationship. You may need to stop complaining about him to others, communicate with him directly and spice up your marriage with more recreational and sexual playtime.

Sunday drives, Saturday walks and even time spent at home can be boring and mundane *or* they can be thrilling, awaited times when you take the initiative to make them playful. Do not wait for him to make all the suggestions, but do the unexpected. Surprise him with lunch at work or better yet, make him come home for lunch and you be the main entrée. That's just a few ways to play!

God is an advocate for phenomenal marital lovemaking. Hebrews 13:4 says, "Marriage is honorable in all and the bed is undefiled." Sexual play should be a delight, not just a duty in a wife's eyes. Men are sensual sexual beings. Married men can be miserable when they are not satisfied and fulfilled by lovemaking's frequency and creativity.

Forgive me, but I naïvely thought that the legal marriage commitment was enough for good Christian men to be happily married although they were sexually dissatisfied. I thought that their spirituality would outweigh the impact of natural desire; however, Holy Spirit quickly corrected me. A husband's commitment to Christ and self-discipline may keep him from seeking sexual fulfillment elsewhere; but, in reality, married men--non-Christian and Christian alike--are extremely miserable when their marriages are not sexually satisfying. Did I say *extremely miserable*? Ouch!

Wives, if you have not been giving your man enough sexual affection and attention, start doing it today. Outwardly express your love for him and don't wait for him to show you affection. When he wants to play with you sexually, you should not have headaches morning, noon and night. Take two aspirins if you feel one coming!

Husbands need their wives to make lovemaking more exciting! Most love it when wives show interest and initiate love-making. Become more adventurous and creative. Stop making love the same old time at the same old place and in the same old position. He may not have told you because he doesn't want to hurt your feelings, but he may be bored in the bedroom. Trying new locations and sexual positions may tickle both of your fantasies. Dare to be different!

Try this wives. Take a day off work or select a Saturday, drop the children off and plan a romantic rendezvous to invest time lavishing eros love on him. Think about making this treat an anticipated monthly date that you both look forward to. His response may pleasantly surprise you!

A sexually playful relationship can make a fun, lasting marriage. Proverbs 5:18-19 is vivid about marital playing. Solomon writes these words of wisdom. "Rejoice with the wife of your youth." "Let her breasts satisfy you at all times," it continues. "And be ravished always with her love." Did you know the Bible had love language like that?

Women, you should no longer underestimate the importance of recreational and sexual play for men. So wives, do not be slack in showing your man attention and affection. The boy inside your man wants to play with you!

Praise. *He needs compliments on his physique and performance.*

Men love to earn and hear their women express praise. Not every woman realizes how powerful her words are in ensuring her man's future success. God designed it so that a woman's voice was the first voice he heard in the womb. His wife should recognize the power of her voice to uplift, encourage and soothe him. She has the potential to catapult him into his destiny like no one else can. The words she speaks and the way she speaks them can help him soar higher than he ever imagined. On the contrary, abusive words can destroy his confidence and make him feel like a failure. Few or no words of praise can stagnate him, too.

Praise requires lots of positive communication, which is essential to the success of any relationship. I believe God wants a man's woman to be his greatest encourager and cheerleader. A woman should always build her man up and never strip his self-esteem with her words or actions.

Every woman should praise her man's physique, his performance and push him to his potential. The truth is that you can't praise a man enough. If you want a man to show off and continue doing something good, make a big deal out of praising him! When he dresses himself well, compliment him on how good he looks and how well coordinated his outfit is. Praise him for being a good provider and when he earns a promotion, degree or brings home a paycheck, praise him. Praise him for taking out the trash or cooking dinner. Praise him for being the man of your dreams. Praise him with your lips, thoughtful gifts and of course, what he likes--lovemaking in marriage!

Praise for a man is like high octane fuel is for a car. It boosts him to higher performance. Every man loves to hear the sound of praise, so a woman should bless her man with sweet words daily. Ladies, do not assume he automatically thinks that today you feel the same way about him as you did yesterday. Assure him of your love through words and deeds and think of fresh new ways to praise him. For example, you can write a love note in the middle of the night and leave it on the mirror for your husband to read as he brushes his teeth in the morning. A personal favorite, putting an unexpected sticky note with a love message under the toilet lid, can quickly become his favorite. That shows a man that you will go to the extremes to say you love him. That praise will really work wonders in his heart!

Just like Jesus loves to hear the sound of your praise, a man loves to hear the sound of his woman's praise. You've likely heard the cliché, "When praises go up, blessings come down." When we praise God privately and publicly we get private and public results. Women get great results when they praise the man God placed in their lives, too.

Quite a few women neglect praise because they think great romantic relationships are solely about what they can receive. God did not leave all relationship maintenance up to the man. In Ephesians 5:33, Apostle Paul tells husbands to love their wives as Christ loved the church and gave Himself for it. Then, he gives specific instruction to the wives to make sure they *respect* and *reverence* their husbands. Properly prioritizing a man over friends, family and children is part of respecting and praising him, too.

Men aim to set themselves up for success and earn praise.

Some women wonder why men specifically ask what they want for Christmas, their birthdays, anniversaries and Valentine's Day. In fact, I've heard women comment about how unromantic they thought that it was when they were asked. Women often want to be surprised, but men want to diminish all chances of their gifts being disliked and rejected and increase their potential to be praised and rewarded. That is why they ask exactly what women want. They do not want to miss an opportunity to be praised!

Don't get upset when he asks what you want. He wants to be sure he pleases you. Every man wants to hit the bullseye with a heartfelt gift so he can hear your praises. Not too many things make him happier than to see the smile on his lady's face and joy in her heart when she receives exactly what she desires. So to be sure that she is pleased and he gets praised, he asks what specific gifts will make her happy. In the meantime, his woman may be upset because she thinks he's not good at guessing and should already know what she wants. He just wants praise!

Women, do you realize that though we think differently, men are very smart? Look at it like this. When a woman goes shopping, her man may stay home or sit on the mall bench. To him, guessing is a waste of time. He doesn't want to waste time or risk her disliking a gift, so he saves time, gets straight to the point and asks what she wants. When he gives her what she wants, he knows he has made her happy and waits to hear her praise him. Women, don't forget to pour the praise on!

A Great Relationship Is Worth The Work!

"A Great Relationship Is Worth The Work" was a very popular message I delivered on my "Spoken Words of Love" radio broadcast. It's a true statement. It requires work to build a great relationship. Women who think love is all about them neglect to give their dates or mates the same attention and affection they want to receive. Sowing sweet love into him can help you reap overflowing returns.

What a powerful force women are in improving their relationships! As the life-changing words of Proverbs 14:1 declare, "A wise woman builds her house, but a foolish one plucks it down with her own hands." So ladies, use your persuasive power to speak life and love into the man in your life who is worthy of your praise. Implement the wisdom of the word of God and woman, build your house!

Song of Solomon's Shulammite lover knew how to build her house. She romanced her man so beautifully that I believe he had no choice but melt in her arms like butter on hot biscuits. That sister paid careful attention to and commented on almost every detail of her man's physique. He observed every fine detail about her, too. Their love talk includes saying that their breath is the scent of apples and their kisses are like the best wine. They talk about the beauty of each other's eyes, teeth, lips, necks, legs and more! It might help you to take notes on their delightful, detailed expressions of admiration and adoration for each other, highlighted in Song of Solomon's eight chapters of vivid imagery and romantic love language. Can you believe that is in the Bible? Grab your Bible and read it!

The drama-free man craves and desperately needs his God-ordained woman's attention, affection and praise. He would rather receive it from her than even think about seeking it elsewhere. The drama-free woman should never minimize the importance of generously sowing seeds of love into the drama-free man who shows he truly cares about her well being.

So ladies, take pride in being his number one love. Take joy in spending time with him and make your time together worth it to him. With gratitude galore, you should shower your man with respect and appreciation, passionately speak life into him and encourage him from the depths of your heart. Wives should lavish love, love, love in the bedroom, too. You be the first one to be sure that you do not leave any voids that any other woman could possibly fill. Love that outstanding man like he needs to be loved publicly and privately. Don't forget to pose, play, and praise!

Every woman must invest in the success of her relationship with her God-ordained man if she wants to have *love without the drama*. When she emphasizes posing for, playing with and praising the man she wants to lead her, listen to her and love her exclusively, their relationship satisfaction can soar. When she reaps the benefits and begins to experience the relationship of her dreams, God's ordained couple will agree that a great relationship really is worth the work!

CHAPTER SIX

Marriage Truths, Myths and Mysteries

God intended marriage to be a demonstration of ministry, not misery.
- Lynetta Jordan

Your love satisfaction impacts overall life satisfaction. The positive emotional impact of marital happiness affects a person's performance in every area. So does the negative impact of marital misery. Every suffering mate is not ready to admit to a miserable marriage, but the truth is the light.

Jesus said that He came that every one of us might have life *and* experience life more abundantly. Abundant means overflowing. Do you believe that His desire for more abundant life for you, expressed in John 10:10, includes a marriage that is overflowing with joy, peace and love? I do.

If you have been bruised, battered and felt defeated in marriage before, may I have the honor of encouraging you? Forgive yourself. You are not a complete failure. Since it took more education to get your driver's license than your marriage license, you could not have possibly known everything you needed to know about being a great mate and having a satisfying, successful marriage. So let's gain more knowledge about God's definition and divine intentions for marriage. Examine your life experiences, too.

A Marriage Is More Than A Beautiful Wedding Day.

Marriage was created by God to be um-um good and it will be um-um good when it's done His way. There are many happy marriages, but in this media and electronic age, bad news seems to sell the most and travel the fastest. We hear more news about failed relationships than successful ones. The 50% divorce rate is highly publicized, but it's rare to hear that the marital success rate is also 50%.

Jesus performed His very first miracle, turning water into wine, at a wedding. As it was then, a wedding celebration is a treasured event for the happy couple where lifetime memories are made for them, family and friends. Most get a sense of joy and delight watching the bridal party walk down the aisle dressed in beautiful, coordinated attire. Tears fly and hearts flutter as couples gaze into each other's eyes, repeat vows and exchange dazzling rings.

But the power of a marriage is not in the cost of the bride's wedding gown, its fabric, beadwork or the length of its train. It's not in the size of a bridal party, the number of guests, the reception location or how many thousands of dollars the entire celebration costs. No, they all pale in comparison to God's true purpose of marriage.

I have seen extravagant, expensive weddings for couples whose marriages did not succeed, so the durability of a marriage cannot be determined at all by the wedding itself. Couples should vow their love exclusively to each other for more than sexual attraction or hope for sexual fulfillment. And they shouldn't plan a wedding just to show off. They should wed because God has predestined them to be one.

If you don't think the body of Christ needs a makeover in understanding the purpose and power of the marriage relationship, it's time to think again. Even before I was 18, God dealt with me heavily about how beautiful He intended marriage to be. I believed that you should not marry any random person because you were a certain age, wanted the thrill of a name change and had no self control. I also believed that marriages needed to be God's perfect will because when you have God's best mate who loves God and you, you have maximum potential for marital fulfillment. As a graduate student in my early 20s, I discovered a book in my aunt's ministry library that elaborated on what the Lord was teaching me. To me, that was more confirmation of God's true desire for marriages.

Many troubled couples perform well on stage, but their marriages are miserable behind the scenes. I have even prayed privately for deliverance in adulterous playboy pastors and other men who have made bold, illicit passes at women and some wives who went astray, too. If some couples you know were honest, they would tell you that they feel like they are dying in miserable marital mistakes. Don't be fooled. Misery is not God's marriage plan at all!

Being a Christian alone does not teach you how to be a mate or solve all marriage problems. Many couples, even in the church, got married for the wrong reasons. Some were pushed to marry people they did not really love as they were encouraged by the "old school" church to marry someone now and learn to love them later. That is living beneath your Christian privilege! God has a greater plan.

Experience Can Be A Tough Teacher.

Experience is one of the toughest teachers you will ever have because the tests are given before the lessons. Many married couples have bumps and bruises from learning by the slow route of trial and error. Honest couples would confess that stumbling while trying to build their marriage has been absolutely frustrating and painful.

God did not intend for marriage to feel like a prison sentence. You and I know a couple or two that are married, but incarcerated. If a few celebrating couples told the truth, their silver anniversary would be equivalent to a 25 year jail term. Like jail, the benefits were guaranteed meals, lighter financial responsibility and the familiarity of a comfort zone. A few imprisoned couples learned to live a dysfunctional lie and publicly pretended like it was normal. Some husbands and wives did get time away from home for work release, but shackles still impeded their advancement and shortened their steps forward in life.

But Lynetta, how can you say that some marriages are like prison sentences when God created marriage and everything God made was good? I'm glad you asked. God created the *institution* of marriage; however, He did not create every marriage and unite every couple we see today. As much as we would like to hope and believe that He did, He did not. (I just felt someone's philosophy shake.) Don't worry, it's not an opinion. The Bible backs this. Psalm 127:1 says, "*Except* the Lord build the house they labor in vain that build it." "*What God has joined together* let not man put asunder," is found in Matthew 19:6. Both denote options.

Please don't twist what I am saying. If you have made a mess by choosing your own will, God still has the power to take your mess and make it a message. Oh yes, He can get good out of any bad situation. However, we, God's people need to get out of the pattern of following our flesh and own wills and afterward asking God to come and bless the messes we made on our own. The best way is God's way. His way is for us to seek Him and ask for His direction first, then obey His instructions. Allowing God to lead and guide you every step of the way into the kingdom mate He has already ordained and created specifically for you will make the rest of your life a whole lot sweeter and easier.

When you settle for less when God wants to bless you with a sizzling relationship, you find out that the tuition at the school of hard knocks is much more than anyone should want to pay. God gives you a choice. You can let the Lord build your relationship (and be like the wise man who built his house upon a rock) *or* build it yourself (like the foolish man who built on the sand and whose house was demolished during a storm). Which do you choose?

God wants you to experience love His way--fulfilling, overflowing and amazing. He did not create marriage to be like a prison sentence, so why live behind bars? Many unequally yoked couples put themselves together and then asked God for His stamp of approval, but that was not His proper order. God's original plan--seeking Him so He can order your steps and connect the right rib to the ribcage it truly fits--was for marriage to be absolutely, positively um-um good!

God Created Marriage, Yet Man Created Some Marriages.

I wholeheartedly agree with the truth and defense that what God has joined together you cannot let man put asunder. Anyone living in or waiting for a God-ordained relationship has learned that you have to invest in, fight for it and protect it. It's scriptural. But what you must be aware of is that just because a minister or priest married a couple, it does not mean that God joined the two of them together. Clergy represent God, but they are not God. You should consult God personally through prayer, then wait for His answer about whether or not you should marry a specific person. God can see farther down the road into your life than you can. He knows if he or she has what you need in your present and also if he or she is capable of walking with you through future challenges, trials and successes.

I hope that your present or future marriage is, but every marriage simply is *not* ordained by the Lord. Quite a few people have gotten married for their own reasons or by the influence of others, not because it was the perfect will of God and part of His divine plan for them to be together.

Some friends or family convinced couples to tie the knot. Some women married to escape their parents' rules. Some were tired of being alone and accepted the first (and worst) offer. They got Bozo instead of Boaz. Some men married the wrong women for public perception after a bruised ego. Some couples married to quench burning flesh and have sex legally. A ticking biological clock sent some searching for a sperm or egg donor. Any reason other than the perfect will and timing of God is the wrong reason to marry.

Tyler Perry's "Why Did I Get Married" play and movies were smashing successes at the box office. So I ask, *why did you get married?* I hope it was because you both knew that God ordained you to marry. If not, was it a result of foolish pride? Were you trying to take revenge on an ex-lover? Was it punishment for a moral crime you committed?

Because two families forced two teens who got pregnant to marry does not mean that God ordained them to be each other's mate. They may have meant well, but their actions to avoid a "bastard baby" could have caused more pain. If you made that mistake as a youth, forgive yourself and those who forced you to marry. Although the pregnancy was unplanned, the baby is not a mistake, but there are consequences of failing to flee fornication as He instructed.

For so long we have played by our own relationship rules not realizing, and in some cases choosing not to acknowledge, that God has a plan for relationship success. Although you are of legal age and big and bad enough to do what you want to do, please think twice before you get married out of spite, anger or any other unorthodox reason. Advise others to do so, too. Not too many people are ready for the suffering and misery they will encounter if it's not God's perfect plan for them to marry the one they are with.

God gives you free will, but it is in your best interest to surrender your will to His perfect will. He knows what is best. You can find yourself happier than you have ever been when you not only acknowledge Him as a church Jesus, but when you humble yourself and let Him lead you in every aspect of choosing and living with your mate.

The Limitations Of A Marriage License

It takes more than a marriage license to keep a couple united and in love. In today's society there are driver's licenses, professional and occupational licenses like real estate and insurance salespersons need and then we have marriage licenses. Most of the previous licenses have to be earned after intense hours of required instruction followed by thorough testing, but not a marriage license. There are no prerequisites. The requirements are be single and of age, pay the fee, get married and obtain the required signatures.

A marriage license is respectable and recognized by law, but the individuals who sign it should acknowledge that its power is limited. Seriously consider the following truths. Get a glass of water. These truths may be tough to swallow.

1. A license means your marriage is legal but it does not certify that your marriage was ordained by God.
2. A marriage license can get you the husband or wife title, but it does not mean that you are well prepared for it.
3. A marriage license does not ensure sexual fidelity.
4. A marriage license alone cannot keep a couple together forever. It can be "cancelled" by annulment or divorce.
5. A marriage license is a legal record, but it doesn't resolve emotional issues or dissolve soul ties or godly bonds.

Are you convinced yet that more than a license is needed to have a great marriage? These facts support the truth that not only do all couples need Jesus to be in the midst of their marriages, but marriages are best when He is the author.

I am sharing raw truth, so I am warning you. I am going to expose more uncooked truths, myths and mysteries that may lump in your throat and knot in your stomach. You may already be appalled that I dared say that some spouses feel like they are locked up and serving jail time. It is the truth. Let me now add that a few miserable mates may describe their marriages as lifetime sentences with death as their only hope for parole. An even more disheartening truth is that some Christian mates feel the same way. Ouch!

A legal marriage is not necessarily a spiritual marriage. I know you may be wondering how that can be true. Here's how. Codes of law are defined by scripture as "the letter." II Corinthians 3:6 says, "The letter kills but the spirit gives life." The law is limited. Just like God created and breathed life into Adam and he became a living soul, He needs to create and breathe life into a marriage for it to flourish.

Even some Christian couples are struggling to survive in dead *legal* marriages that have never had *spiritual life* because they were not ordained by God. You can seek a *general* mate, but God wants you to have the *specific* mate He created just for you so you can have all of His benefits. Don't you want your marriage thrive, not just survive?

God wants us to view marriage on His higher level. It is supposed to be beneficial and add to your love, joy, peace and happiness, but when you settle and marry outside His will, you don't receive His full benefit package. Man-made marriage is more like a prison sentence than a blessing.

Every marriage was not "made in heaven." God united some couples. Others united themselves. They may have gotten married with good intentions; however, they are frustrated after authoring their own relationship. Then they asked the Lord to approve the script they chose to write on their own. God can help you go through, but you will not be happy when you are not with His divine mate for you.

A self-selected marriage is like going to the mountains for vacation when you originally desired to go to the ocean. It's still a vacation, but those two totally different locations with completely different scenery are no comparison at all. Though you can try to make the most out of it and still have a good time, you may still be quite disappointed because it's not the type of fun you expected. Oceans and mountains are two totally different environments!

It's time for an honest, personal and confidential reality check-up today. If you are dating or married, here is your check-up question. Has your experience with the person you are presently with been a big let down--a lot less than what you expected? There several possible reasons for a "Yes" answer. It could be you. He or she could have pretended to be different before you married. It may be because you missed a big warning sign or chose not to see it. It might be because that is not your God-ordained mate.

Brothers, can you look in the mirror and honestly say, "She brings out the best in me and makes me happier than I ever imagined I would be?" You might not have your true rib if you can't. Sisters, can you look in the mirror and honestly say that man brings out the best in you and your kingdom connection is so strong you can feel it? If not, you might be dangling and hanging on to the wrong ribcage.

A legal marriage is limited, but God-ordained couples are empowered to survive relationship storms. A familiar parable, Matthew 7:24-27, talks about the foundations on which houses are built. The wise build upon a rock, but the foolish upon sand. Regardless of where a home is built, storms will arise and test the foundation's strength. Storms test relationships, too. Those that are God-ordained and rooted and grounded in Christ, the solid rock, can weather the fiercest storms. When you examine a storm's aftermath, you will know if your love was built upon a rock or sand.

Song of Solomon 8:7, "Many waters cannot quench love; neither can the floods drown it," is one of the scriptures I clung to when I had to stand on His promises through a severe love storm. Life and the enemy will send storms to test and try relationships. Trials will wash puppy love and infatuation away, but real love stands, endures and outlasts storms. In fact, storms work in real love's favor, connecting the couple and causing their love to strengthen and deepen in a dimension that could not be achieved any other way.

Satan is constantly trying to detour and disconnect people from their destined mates because he knows how powerful a God-ordained marriage is. Where there is unity there is strength and if one can chase a thousand, two can put ten thousand enemies to flight. Two united people walking in spiritual and natural accord are a fierce weapon to Satan's kingdom. Hell cannot stand that! It's time for couples with kingdom assignments to be steadfast and unmovable as I Corinthians 15:58 says. Satan knows, but you need to realize how powerful a kingdom marriage is.

What Is A Wife?

Proverbs 18:22 states, "He that finds a wife finds a good thing and obtains the favor of the Lord." That is so true; however, there are more qualifications than being at least an 18 year old female to be a man's true *spiritual* wife. A marriage certificate can name her a man's legal spouse, but that does not mean she is God's ordained wife for him--his "good thing" that will bring him the full favor of the Lord.

Raging hormones and burning flesh can lead a man to seek and marry a female for sexual gratification who lacks what is needed for his personal, sexual and overall life satisfaction. You should pause, read that sentence again and meditate on it. Yes, church folk, it's better to marry than to burn, but it's worse to be outside God's perfect will.

A friend in ministry recently preached that some delay their destinies by making a pit stop a permanent dwelling. A woman may be a decent *girlfriend* to a man in transition, but not be chosen and prepared by God to be *his wife*. Marrying a *good woman* still does not make her *God's wife*.

A woman should not first become a wife when she says vows and signs a marriage certificate. She should be a wife prior to becoming legal. By wife, I don't mean that she is a woman who was married to someone else first. I mean she should be a woman who has God's character and who has been specially prepared by Him to help a specific man enjoy and maximize his life and help propel him to his destiny. She should *accelerate*, not just *assist* him in future endeavors. The real wife has been empowered by God to speak life into her man. Her inspiration will be undeniable!

While working around the house one day, God spoke a powerful revelation to me about the contrast between a *woman* and a *wife*. I share this profound revelation straight from His heavenly throne to you. Holy Spirit spoke to me that there is an often overlooked distinction between those two terms. Any *woman* may *assist* a man, but only his true, God-ordained *wife* is fully capable of being his *helpmate*.

Men, God's true wife for you will be more than your *assistant*, but she will be your *helpmate*. Some men, He explained, are married to good housekeepers who do assist them with sexual needs and lighten their load at home with the children, their businesses and even in their ministries, but all of these women are not these men's God-ordained helpmates, their true kingdom companions.

Let me share with you the rest of His explanation. An *assistant* follows instructions of her leader and is rewarded to do what is asked of her. But a *helpmate* is so much greater than an assistant because a helpmate is thinking about what a man needs before he even realizes he needs it. Because a man's true helpmate knows him so intimately and deeply--she knows his thoughts, secrets, fears and even his reasoning behind why he does things the way he does them--she prepares the way and makes it easier for him to advance into greater success than he ever imagined. Literally, he was limited in the amount of favor he could obtain without his true wife. She lovingly covers him in demon trembling, effectual and fervent prayer. Proverbs 31:10 says, "Who can find a virtuous woman, for her price is far above rubies?" *God's wife* is a man's priceless blessing!

What Is A Husband?

It takes more than a penis, testicles, chest and facial hair to make a male a responsible man. Being responsible does not necessarily make a man a good, loving husband either.

God needs men to seek Him first and let Him prepare and teach them how to be great husbands to their divine wives. One of the Bible's greatest instructions for them, found in Ephesians 5:25, is for husbands to love their wives as Christ loved the church and gave Himself for it.

Seriously think about this. A man may give good sex; however, how can He give good *love* if He is not in love with Jesus? A deeper relationship with Christ--which is more than religious or denominational devotion--increases a man's capacity to love his wife. A man cannot give any woman his best when he does not love the Lord, for He is the One who teaches us all how to truly love and forgive. So if you know a man who wants or needs to love his wife better, he should seek and pursue loving the Lord more.

God also wants men to seek Him to find the one specific woman He created "from his rib" to be his helpmate. Too many men do not consult and listen to Him before they marry. A man should not assume a woman is God's choice for him because she is meek, makes him feel needed or does everything that he says with no questions. Some initially choose naïve, unchallenging women on purpose, often as psychological protection and pain prevention. But those men become bored, disgruntled and miserable in unfulfilling relationships because they are not connected to their God-ordained spouses, their kingdom companions.

Men, did you know that your God-ordained wife is your assignment from God *and* that she is a significant part of you obediently fulfilling your purpose and divine calling? Many men miss that fact. "Assignment" doesn't mean that loving her has to be a hard task. Nor does it mean she has to be a woman with an obvious problem. She may be a self-assured woman who needs to be wrapped in the arms of a loving man who whispers sweet words of love in her ear and tells her how precious she is to God and him. God will use Him to motivate her and bless them both to accomplish more together than each did alone. Future husbands, the best advice I can give you is to follow God's leading all the way to the specific woman He has assigned you to uplift, nurture, cover, love and be His reflection. *God's wife* will do you good and not evil all the days of your life.

Finally men, don't let the flesh traps trick you because it takes more than sex to make a marriage. Proverbs 23:27 warns of loose women. Some twenty-first century women will "wiggle the bait" to catch a "paid" man. They will use Delilah-like tactics to ensnare men and lead them into marriage, but that's out of God's order. Her catching him does not mean that he is her God-ordained husband either.

Men, beware of charming, enticing Delilahs, like Samson faced in Judges 16, who have impure motives. Their fleshly fantasies may delay destiny or ultimately destroy you. The thief steals, kills and destroys, but Jesus came for us to have life more abundantly. So why not have it more abundantly in relationships? When a man pursues and marries his God-ordained bride, his true missing rib, he can.

Marriage Is About Ministry, Not Misery.

God wants to saturate your life with love. He prepared *His mate* for you to help catapult you into your destiny and make life more joyful than ever. God wants that for you. His desire is for marriage to be exciting for years to come and that there be increasing anticipation and expectation daily. However, marrying the wrong person can slow your progress, make you feel like you are in a tailspin or wasting time circling the airport when you are past due to land.

Marriage really is ministry. That's a message I delivered on a live radio broadcast. It's right in I Corinthians 7:34. "The unmarried cares for the things of the Lord, how she may please the Lord, but a married woman is concerned on how she may please her husband." If you are married, your spouse is your first ministry, so do not neglect your home.

Effective ministry is targeted and specific. Effective ministry abounds with unconditional love. But, effective ministry will also be challenged. As in ministry, sometimes couples have to deal with conflict, grief and painful blows. Many couples were hurt in the process of living and learning by trial and error and realized the right way to handle each other *after* doing some things the wrong way.

You may be married and more frustrated than ever right now. If you went ahead of God or against His leading, are unequally yoked and not married to your God-ordained mate, you have definitely suffered. But have hope. Trouble does not last always. Do not disbelieve God's dream about marriage just because you are not living it yet. Believe that God designed marriage to be about ministry, not misery.

God expects husbands and wives minister to each other regularly sexually. I Corinthians 7:3-5 says that husbands and wives should render due benevolence to each other. They should recognize that their bodies belong to their spouses and willingly make love often. Lovemaking should be gladly looked forward to with your God-ordained mate.

A husband should also take note of the importance and seriousness of treating his wife well. In Ephesians 5, Apostle Paul instructs husbands to love wives as Christ loved the church and to love them as their own selves. I Peter 3:7 admonishes men to give honor to wives *so that their prayers will not be hindered.* That sounds clear to me.

A godly wife must be sure to minister to her husband in the specific ways he needs to be ministered to. In Ephesians 5:33, Apostle Paul gives wives one instruction, to see that they reverence their husbands. I love The Amplified Bible's crystal clear interpretation of that verse. It reads, "And let the wife see that she respects and reverences her husband, that she notices him, regards him, honors him, prefers him, venerates and esteems him, and that she defers to him, praises him, and loves and admires him exceedingly." How can you misunderstand that? It's time to work on it wives! He needs your respect as much as you need his love.

To have love that grows and continues to flourish as the years progress, couples must sacrifice self-centeredness to constantly think of ways they can better minister to each other. Before a couple decides to marry, they both need to consider if they are able and willing to live up to these duties. Ministry is a sacrifice. Marriage really is ministry.

Marriage Myths and Mysteries

A couple's marital joy should last beyond their wedding day. Whether you have been married for years or are currently single and waiting for God's ordained mate, knowing the truth can help make your future brighter than your past. After reading this chapter, you may realize that you had some misconceptions about what marriage truly is. So let me expose more marriage myths and mysteries.

Myth 1: Marriage will resolve all of your personal issues.

> Marriage will not resolve your issues. In fact, it will magnify them. Then you will affect and possibly infect your spouse with your poisonous attitude. You need to get alone with God individually to work on resolving personal issues. When two people with major issues marry they create larger issues!

Myth 2: Marriage will emotionally fulfill you.

> Marriage is meant to be fulfilling, but putting the pressure on a spouse to make you happy is not healthy or realistic. Even if he or she does make you happy, he or she can't give you lasting true joy. Some voids only Jesus can fill. Legally married people can still feel alone and misunderstood.

Myth 3: You are not a complete person without a mate.

> You don't need to be married to feel validated when God validates you. You are already valuable to Him!

Myth 4: Marriage fixes your relationship's dating problems.

Though your expectations of marriage and the husband and wife title are great, that will not fix your problems. If you marry the wrong person, you will have more problems than when dating. If he or she was unaffectionate, unclean, stingy, verbally abusive or had any other undesirable trait before you married, guess what. It will likely still be that way. In fact, it may be worse because you married him or her without requiring him or her to be better.

Myth 5: If he/she is not what you want, change him/her.

You can't make a person what he or she is not. Finding someone of the opposite sex who needs a little sprucing up or cheer may not be the best idea. It may boost your ego, but when that high wears off you may be stuck with someone you don't desire. Wait until they are more mature or healed before you date them. It's a whole lot easier to "train" children than adults. If you need a fix-up project, try painting, reupholstering or a hobby. Don't try love.

Mystery 1: Marriage should be 50/50.

Marriage should be 100/100, requiring 100% effort from both. It should have two emotionally complete, independent (not codependent) individuals who become interdependent. Both spouses must give their all to have a successful and healthy marriage.

Mystery 2: Any female can be a wife.

A man has freewill and can legally marry any woman; however, he should be advised that every woman is not a wife. Neither is every woman *his* wife. Signing a legal document is a contract. It's limited. It may change her last name, but it does not necessarily change her heart toward you. Men, when you have the wrong rib in the place where only your true missing rib fits, your heart can be punctured.

Mystery 3: Any man can be a husband.

A woman has free will, so she can marry any man that is willing to marry her. However; every man is not a husband. A woman must know that although he may be a good provider or have nice things, it does not mean that he is chosen by God to be *her* husband. Just like God has to prepare a woman to be a wife, He must prepare and mature a man before he becomes a husband to his God-ordained mate.

Mystery 4: A legal marriage is strong enough to keep a couple faithful to one another and in love forever.

Marriage is a recognized legal status, but its purpose is beyond legal sex and having babies. God created marriage to be a spiritual and natural relationship with the mate He predestined for you. Legal contracts can be dissolved. Partnerships end. Businesses close. A *legal only* marriage may not last.

Mystery 5: Since marriage was God's original idea, every existing marriage was predestined by Him.

God did not unite every couple. Although a minister may have performed a Christian ceremony, every existing marriage has not been ordained by God. Psalms 127:1, "Except the Lord build the house, they labor in vain that build it," presents two relationship building options. You can build it or wait on God to build it. When the Lord builds a relationship, your labor and whatever you encounter or endure will not be in vain. But when you attempt on your own to construct something that will ultimately fall, it results in great suffering. Some couples did not wait on the Lord, but chose to put themselves together. When you marry your kingdom mate, you can both joyfully sing the words of Psalm 118:23, "This is the Lord's doing and it is marvelous in our eyes!"

Mystery 6: Christian marriages do not have to be or need to be intimate, romantic and sexually satisfying.

Christian marriages should be the most intimate since God authored marriage. Jesus was the Bible's only person birthed by a virgin. The rest were born after couples "knew" each other. Hebrews 13:4 says that the marriage bed is undefiled. It is a shame that some married couples make less love now than when they were dating and disobedient. Ouch! Tighten up Christian mates. Fully enjoy God's gift!

God's Mysterious Revelation Of "The Right Rib"

I cannot stress enough how important it is for a man to have his right rib. Husbands, being married to *the right rib* serves a divine purpose. God gave me a phenomenal revelation about the rib's purpose. I hope it blesses you.

First, He talked to me about the body's anatomy. In the natural, the ribs extend from the side to the front. They are positioned just right to function as protection for the heart and lungs, both major organs. Lungs represent breath and the heart is the center of life. The Lord revealed to me that His God-ordained wife is the perfect fit for her husband's ribcage. *The right rib* is divinely positioned to protect and preserve her husband's breath and life. Like the wife in Proverbs 31:12, she will do him good and no evil forever.

A rib that doesn't fit will loosely protect the heart and lungs. When either is punctured, a person can die quickly. In fact, *the wrong rib* can puncture what God created *the right rib* to protect. Did you get that revelation? Marrying *the wrong rib* can knock a man's wind out and cause his heart to bleed. Seriously, internal injuries lead to death.

What God has joined together, let not man put asunder. A God-ordained marriage is a precious gift from the Lord. If you know you are married to your kingdom companion, the mate God created especially for you, do not take your God-given love for granted. Some people become boring spouses after they settle in marriage. Don't be married and lazy. Celebrate your spouse and work on increasing your love and building dreams daily. Then *the right rib* and the right ribcage may have and enjoy *love without the drama*.

CHAPTER SEVEN
Wisdom For The Single and Seeking

Even when you are living single, it is wise to prepare for marriage.
- Lynetta Jordan

Have you been waiting to meet and marry the right one? If you have waited this long, why would you stop short of your true blessing by settling for someone who is not what you have been waiting for? It may seem like a long wait, but you are closer now than ever before. If you are anxious because your biological clock is ticking, remember that God made the clock. Waiting for God's chosen mate brings a worthwhile blessing. He makes the right spouse worth it!

Taking time to pray and prepare when waiting and dating will increase your chances of having *love without the drama* in marriage. Regardless of a wedding's size or cost, exchanging vows and signing a marriage license do not automatically ensure marital success. It will be a tragedy to marry outside God's perfect will and then feel alone with a mate or wish you were single again when you lack needed and expected affection and support from your spouse. You see, while so many singles are waiting to get married, much too many married people are wishing they were single again. It's true. Remembering this will comfort and encourage you as try to wait patiently for your future mate!

Right Companionship Is God's Plan

No matter what your age, you should not be ashamed of your desire to be married--for the right reasons, of course. Whether never married, widowed, separated or divorced, the majority of single men and women do desire delightful companionship. Proverbs 18:22 states that, "He that finds a wife finds a good thing and obtains the favor of the Lord." Ecclesiastes 4:9-10 says, "Two is better than one. If they fall, the one shall lift up the other." So don't let anyone fool you or make you miss a blessing. God's plan for you includes marrying His ordained mate for you at His appointed time.

It is much easier to share the weight of life's load with the right person than to have to handle it solo. I don't know many people who prefer to carry life's burdens alone. Though many successfully manage the personal and financial responsibilities of a household singlehandedly, most do it because they have to rather than want to. By no choice of their own, many women and some men have been forced to become head of household and raise children on their own. Single parent household statistics continue to climb, especially in minority communities. This book is one of my contributions to the healing and stability of individuals and families worldwide.

As God observed His marvelous creation in Genesis 2, He saw that Adam was alone though the creatures had mates. God performed holy surgery, took Adam's rib and created Eve, a helpmeet suitable for him. Eve was not just Adam's eye candy, but she was there to help him and add to Adam's enjoyment of life. They were a divine team.

God's divine, created purpose for woman includes *helping* her God-ordained husband. No matter how single and satisfied a woman is, she will be most fulfilled in partnership with her true mate. Strong, independent, career-oriented women may be blessed and confident without a man; however, they should not forget that it was God's original idea and plan for a woman to *help,* to come alongside and assist, her God-ordained husband. Not just any man will complete her though. She needs the man God formed her for and from. When she connects with her "true ribcage" they will be a perfect fit, capable of experiencing total fulfillment and true *love without the drama.*

Especially during my teenage years, my parents emphasized the importance of making good decisions on my own. I clearly recall them saying, "We have to teach you how to make good decisions because we will not always be with you. But if we teach you *how* to make them, then you can make right choices on your own."

Everyone has daily decisions to make. Some decisions, like choosing the right shoes to match your attire, will not make or break you (although some may disagree). Others, like deciding who to marry, are much more life-impacting. Wisdom says that you should meditate longer when contemplating major decisions. These choices affect you forever, therefore they should not be finalized in a few minutes, but require wise counsel, prayer and preparation. The decision to pursue a relationship with a person of the opposite sex who has some of the qualities you desire, but is not the total package of what you need is *settling.*

You Don't Have To Be A Desperately Seeking Single.

Some persons think that being married to somebody, even if it's not the right somebody, is better than not being married at all. I wholeheartedly disagree. Many Christians act like God has not considered their companionship, so they desperately search for it on their own. They encounter setbacks and extra heartbreak on their own journeys when God wants to make it easier. Think about it. If God planned every other detail about your life, why would He omit your love life? He just wants you to obey and get in position.

Some members of the body of Christ have dysfunctional views of marriage and dating. As a singles minister in my 20s, God revealed to me that He has created a specific mate for all who are destined to be married. I expressed this revelation of a God-ordained mate in a conversation with a married pastor. This Christian leader's unspiritual response baffled me. He replied, "But do you have time to wait on God to find your mate?" That opened my eyes to see that Christian leaders can also miss God's mark in relationships.

When you choose to date or marry an incomplete package--perhaps under the influence of lust, family or peer pressure, emotional hurt, frustration, anger, revenge, low self-esteem, impatience and unwillingness to "wait for the promise"--you are compromising the promise of God. The results of compromise can cause you severe heart pain.

When we settle for less than God's best, we drastically decrease our chances of having gratifying, successful love. God's desire is for our relationships, especially marriages, to sizzle. In case life hasn't already taught you, let me tell you that relationships soon fizzle when you settle for less!

Have you ever opened the Bible to a random page and your eyes zeroed in on a specific scripture that you had never seen or heard before? Then, when you read it, you felt like God put it in the Bible just for you. That's what happened to me the first time I read Proverbs 24:27. I absolutely have to share it with you. The Amplified Bible's version says, "Put first things first. Prepare your work outside and get it ready for yourself in the field; and afterward build your house and establish a home."

I was floored! God gave me a clear direction so I would not have to be anxious about when I would get married. The scripture told me to prepare myself as an individual first--go to college, establish my career, business and ministry--and after that then I will build a physical house and establish a home (a sizzling, loving marriage). If I followed His instruction and busied myself with striving for these goals before marriage, I would not have time to be a desperately seeking single. I also realized that I would have something to offer the man of my dreams. He might just notice and pursue me as I was doing all of that work!

There is a reason for your season of singleness, too. His grace will enable you to be content in whatever state you are in, so relax. God has kingdom work for you to do while you are waiting to be divinely connected with His ordained mate. I Corinthians 7:32 and 34 tell us that the unmarried are to tend to things of the Lord. While you are still single, pour your energy into serving the Lord while you wait for God's mate. So I ask, what have *you* done for Jesus lately?

Pursue Your Purpose As You Prepare For Marriage.

It is extremely important for singles to pursue their individual purposes while they wait to meet and marry God's chosen mate. What are your goals and dreams? There is a Chinese proverb that says, "The journey of a thousand miles begins with a single step." What steps are you currently taking toward fulfilling them so you can see them manifest in your future?

You are an important part of God's plan. What do you feel God has created and gifted you to do? It may be the thing you like to do the most or that is easiest for you. If you have not thought about that before, now is the perfect time to meditate on it. Make it a top priority to take time to ask the Lord what specific role He created you to fill in the world. In addition, search online or in the library for one of many assessments designed to help determine your leadership abilities, learning style and spiritual gifts. It's amazing what you can learn about yourself!

Be very passionate about life while you are living single! Don't let life and time pass you by because you are waiting to get married before you do anything significant. You do not have to wait until you get married to become adventurous. Learn to love yourself before you invest all your time loving someone else. Your single season is the time to go out and explore the world! Go on a cruise or vacation, purchase a home, buy your own car or SUV, obtain higher education, apply for your dream job, move to another city, write a book, record a CD or start a new business. Whatever your dream is, pursue it NOW!

I know God has called and chosen me to encourage every single woman and ensure her that God has great blessings planned for her even before she gets married. Isaiah 54:5 says, "Thy maker is thy Husband." God, your first husband, is jealous over you. Ladies, He wants to set the example of how you are to be provided and cared for so you can recognize and appreciate the man He sends. He does not want you to be mishandled by any earthly man or idolize any earthly man over Him either. Do not let limited thinking make you miss what the Lord wants to do for you as your first love and husband while you wait for the physical man to show up on the stage of your life.

I drove by a church billboard that said, "When God is all you have, you have all you need." Single women listen. Prior to marriage, God blessed me to pursue higher education, earn Bachelor's and Master's degrees, purchase and keep my own brand new home and first new car, plus start my own business without anyone's help but His. In fact, I birthed my business during unemployment. I did not have a business mentor. I did not have any savings left. I could not even find any investors. I did not have a sugar daddy on the side who gave me money. God kept making ways for me during tough times and I refused to start living a compromised Christian lifestyle. In fact, I believe God blessed me beyond myself because I trusted, leaned and depended totally on Him for everything. He made sure no one but Him would get credit for my supernatural success. All of these things were beyond my dreams! He rewarded me because I diligently sought Him.

God has His best prepared for you to possess *before* you have a mate. I had no idea what God could do for me solo. I really didn't. But His love and confidence in me was greater than any finances I needed or belief I had in myself.

God manifested my blessings in the midst of deep valleys. So let me encourage you ladies. Do not miss any blessing God wants to give you because your mind tells you not to expect any significant treasures until you are married. If God opens a door for you to invest in your future by purchasing rather than renting a home, buy one. Go a little farther. Learn how to invest and buy a few more.

I am a living testimony that God will bless and prosper you while you are single. Forget the haters who said that I must have had a man funding me somewhere. I did! God was that man! When you know His good love, you will be ready for the man He created you specifically for. At God's appointed time, He will send His man to shower you with more of His everlasting good love. You will feel God loving you through the earthly man He sends to be your husband!

Don't worry. Owning your home, car, business or jewelry as a single woman does not mean you do not need a man. It shows your confidence in God and yourself. It will not decrease your chances of getting married--unless you count the elimination of the wrong men who want unchallenging women with minimum goals. At times you are surrounded by them. A confident man will be drawn to you, but bums will stay away! This increases your opportunity to marry a brother who is not lazy, but striving for and achieving excellence in his life. Don't settle for less!

Be What You Want To Receive In Your Dream Mate.

"A virtuous and worthy wife (earnest and strong in character) is a crowning joy to her husband, but she who makes him ashamed is as rottenness in his bones." That's how the Amplified Bible translates Proverbs 12:4. As a woman thinks about what kind of future wife she wants to be, she needs to assess who she is and how she acts right now. Who she is now is a reflection of who she will attract.

If you want a drama-free date or mate, you have to let go of the drama in your own life. During my high school years I got excited about God. I believed that all things truly were possible with Him and wanted His best of everything. I clearly remember hearing God speak to me then, "If you want to have a king, you must be a queen." I learned that I must choose to be virtuous and act like a royal child of the King. I must teach others how to treat me.

We often avoid thinking of our personal responsibility in attracting a date or mate. If you continue to attract the wrong type of dates, you need to take a deeper look into yourself. If you have been disappointed, you may need to examine what kind of vibes are radiating from you. For example, if all these men seem to want is sex ladies, it is possible that you are dressing too provocatively or acting desperate. Are you wearing your emotions on your sleeve? If so, men can smell a woman's need or desire for male attention. That's when a woman has to discern what's what and who's who, so she knows if a man is the counterfeit, only appearing to take advantage of her loneliness, or the real prince coming to carry her away into her dreams.

Does Opposite Attraction Bring Satisfaction?

I ministered the message, "Your Mate Is Your Mirror," during a singles ministry radio broadcast years ago. The Lord revealed to me that ultimately, you will attract someone who has similar characteristics as you. Most of those will be internal traits. He or she does not have to look like you outwardly, but there will likely be strong similarities in your character, strengths, weaknesses and personalities, perhaps just revealed in different ways.

You have heard it said that opposites attract. You may even believe it. Think about it. Opposites may attract, but do they make the best lifetime mates? Some areas of opposite attraction are understandable and impact overall marital satisfaction in minor ways. Some differences have a slim probability of making or breaking a relationship; for example, if he is outgoing and she is soft-spoken, if she is five feet tall and he is six feet tall, if he is an outdoorsman while she prefers indoor activities. However, in order to have peaceful and successful long-term relationships, it is extremely important to have core values in common.

When you assess who you are--your life expectations and what you bring to the marriage table--you are more likely to know if a date is a realistic match. Relationships where the man and woman have strongly differing core values--perceived marital roles and expectations, parenting strategies and religious beliefs and practices--rarely last forever. Do not lower your standards or alter your personality to accommodate a date. If you compromise in hopes of keeping anything, you will not. You will lose it.

What Do You Desire In Your Drama-Free Dream Mate?

Do you want an encore of your past relationship drama? Was it a tragic or comedic performance? When reflecting on past romantic relationships and friendships, most people do not want their scarred history of unfaithfulness, rejection and compromise repeated. I have great news. Your relationship destiny does not have to repeat your history! Though your past may have been painful, there are better days ahead. The view from your windshield (looking ahead) is much broader than your rear view mirror (looking behind). Your future is brighter than your past!

It's a common saying that history repeats itself, but it is not necessarily true. Your future relationships can mimic your past mistakes, but they do not have to. It's your choice. Choosing your dates wisely and not settling for less than you deserve and desire will increase your chances of meeting and marrying your predestined, drama-free mate.

Dating is an interview for more long term commitment. Considering each date as a potential mate may change the way you view dating. You may or may not be entertaining the idea of marriage when you first meet them, but that does not mean that they are not considering marrying you.

You have likely learned how to make better dating and marriage decisions after stumbling through past trials and errors. In addition, your observation of other couples has helped you more clearly define what you do and don't want in your marriage. From these experiences, you should now know what you can live with and what you can no longer live without. So let's talk about personal preferences.

A Special Order Relationship

Let's say you need a new car. When you go on the car lot and you have no idea of what specific make, model, or color you want, they will try to sell you anything you qualify for. Although you can afford it and will be excited about driving a shiny new car off the lot, you may later discover that you are unhappy with several of its features. Why? When you aren't clear on what you want or settle for less than your heart's desire, it leads to dissatisfaction.

All transportation is not the same. When I go car shopping, I have already studied the specific vehicle that I desire. I tell the salesperson what interior and exterior color and features I want. When he offers me a different color or car, I will not buy it. I am determined to be 100% satisfied!

The last car I purchased had to be shipped from an out of state dealership. I test drove a similar one nearby, but it was not *the* one. The exterior was red, but the interior was not what I desired, so I continued to search near and far until I found exactly what I wanted. Only two cars in the entire USA met my qualifications. I waited, but seeing my new car with my license plate on the showroom floor was well worth the wait. And it was shipped for free!

I waited to get the exact car I wanted because waiting guaranteed me satisfaction. Misery is something I can't live with easily, but I know people who live in miserable relationships daily. Marriage is about ministry, not misery. I know you can have the kind of love you want when you prepare, wait and know *your* investment before you sign your name on the dotted line. That's why I wrote this book!

Your God-ordained mate is a divine special order. He or she is made to your specific preferences. That takes time. Whether you go to a fast food or a classy sit down restaurant, it takes additional preparation time when you order a meal a different way than it is usually prepared. Whether it is pepper and mayo only, add cheese, no pickles or another special way, the desired flavor is worth the wait!

So have you been wondering why you are still single? God is making sure your future mate has all the right ingredients, is properly prepared and fully cooked before He serves him or her to you. Your job is to sit, rest, relax and enjoy yourself at God's table while you wait on Him to serve you His prepared blessing that is sure to delight you.

If you feel like you have been waiting an extra long time, think about a meal's preparation process. Steak and high quality meats are better slow-cooked than microwaved. If cooked too fast, the texture will be too rubbery and dry to eat and enjoy. So stop stressing. Quality takes time.

Please don't go ahead of God and get a substitute mate. If you get a substitute instead of God's real one you will be disappointed. Sugar and sweet-n-low are both sweeteners, but their tastes are distinctly different. Too much of the substitute is unpleasant. One cup of sugar is tasty in tea, but one cup of sweet-n-low is overwhelmingly bitter!

Let God fully prepare your mate. Like chocolate cake, you want a sweet, completely cooked and cooled mate, not a half-baked one. Trying to enjoy him or her raw is a severe health risk. Let God's fire burn out impurities and flaws. Then, when He serves your love to you, you can enjoy!

Physical Characteristics

What do you desire in your future spouse? How much does a prospective mate's physical characteristics matter to you? That varies by individual. Only you know what you can open your eyes and smile at when you wake up.

You know your dream's imagined physical features--complexion, hair color and length, height and body structure--that you replay in your mind's video. But the Lord and I need you to think about something. You see, we do not want you to overlook a priceless diamond because the box is not wrapped the way you thought it would be.

Men, will you miss a great woman if she is shaped more like a two liter than a 16oz coke bottle? Ladies, will you overlook that man if he is not as tall, dark and handsome as you expected? She may not be 36-24-36. He might not be 6-6-6 yet--six feet tall with a six pack abdomen and a six figure salary. But be careful not to miss your divine mate!

It is fine to dream, but do not forget the omnipotence and omniscience of your God. Paint your own picture, but know that God can have a sense of humor. She may have all of the inward traits you asked for but not look like you dreamed she would. He may be shorter and lighter and make less money than you imagined. His or her age may be younger or older than you thought, but a person who is younger can be wiser and more mature than some older ones. It all depends on life experiences and time with God.

God knows what you like and will not disappoint you. He also knows what you can handle. Believe that God can and will make His relationship dreams for you come true!

Don't Date Potential. Date Reality.

It seems crazy to squeeze a tart lemon and expect to get sweet orange juice doesn't it? But that's what singles often do in dating. They believe the best and ignore the reality of who a date really is on the inside. They hope for sweetness when evidence shows that the inside is tart. Yet, they keep squeezing and hoping that what comes out will change.

An extremely important question to ask is if you can live happily with a mate if his or her unproductive habits, attitudes, religious views and moral values never change. So many singles expect that their dates will make positive changes and become all they ever dreamed they would be the moment that they marry them. You may think that your love is powerful enough to make your date want to change, but ultimately, that decision to change is up to him or her. Do not expect marriage to give you a new and improved version of your current date. It usually won't.

Believing in potential without acknowledging the truth is a big error singles make. If someone tells you they only want you for sex, believe them. If someone tells you about a bad habit or negative trait they have, believe them. If a person acts uncouth when you are dating, believe that that is who they really are. Decide then if that is what you want in your future. Don't settle for less than what matters most.

I'm reminded of the story of the man who found a snake shivering. He picked it up, took it home and wrapped it in a blanket. When the snake recovered, it bit the man. He was startled. He asked the snake why he bit someone who was so kind to him. He replied, "Biting is what snakes do."

I am a positive and optimistic person. Because of my great faith, I like to look beyond the present moment and envision a brighter future. That works great for personal goals, but when determining whether a date will be a great future mate, it is important to look at reality. It's dangerous to deny it. Take a good look at your date's present habits, ambition, drive and determination. Is he or she energized and in hot pursuit of life? Or is he or she satisfied with the daily humdrum, having little vision for a more lucrative and fulfilling life. If your date is lazy now, don't make the mistake of assuming he or she will become more motivated later. Talk can be cheap and actions speak louder than words, so pay close attention to your date's current actions and how long it takes him or her to follow-up on his or her words. Optimistic people believe their love will inspire others to want more and to do better. It can, but that does not always happen. It is dangerous to ignore a date's reality. Walk spiritually by faith, but **do not date by faith!**

I am not embarrassed to say that I wasted time dating by faith. I had dinner with an academic acquaintance who valued education, had a good work ethic, a neat personal appearance and was raised in church. We were very casual and I had not even thought about dating him, but I remember when the Lord led me to ask him if he thought he had a calling on his life. He admitted it and shared heartwarming life stories about God's undeniable presence. A man's spiritual values are top priority, so after this, he became more attractive to me. I just knew that since this man had a calling on his life, he would want to walk it out.

I held on to his potential and my hope that he would turn around and become a fanatic for Christ like me too long. I fasted and prayed specifically for God to deal with his heart. God did, but the decision to sell out completely to God was this man's, not my decision to make. He got close; however, he chose not yield. I remember the day he said he *thought* about going ahead and giving in (to Christ). But he chose to hold on to what was more familiar, the world. Finally, he disrespected me. God helped me let go.

Men and women get excited in the initial dating stage. After a few conversations (the impressing stage), it is easy, especially for women, to wrap yourself in a loved one's hopes and dreams. It is good to see who someone could become with God, but know that without that person's cooperation and personal motivation, that will not happen. Do not date people with potential and try to save them. It might make you feel good to think you can help bring them into God's kingdom, but you cannot make them love God genuinely. They have to surrender to Him on their own.

It is sad to report that some Christians, even those who serve as leaders, attend church and Bible Study weekly, have refused to let God lead their love lives and build their relationships. They have slammed the door in God's face, shut their spiritual and natural ears, ignored His voice and ran their own way to chase after dates and mates. Some of them thought they could choose on their own, then bring the date or mate to God and expect Him to approve their choices. Not so. God should call the shots when you are looking for love. Are you letting Him lead your dating life?

The Spiritual Aspect Of Dating

Have you ever been guilty of almost losing your identity and letting your relationship with God slip when focusing on loving someone? It can happen quicker than you think. If you go over the deep end when dating, you may not be ready for your mate yet. God wants you to be mature enough to be balanced. Exalting him or her as an idol and neglecting God and yourself is love mismanagement. He created us for true companionship, but He wants us to be able to manage it. If you are in a rush to get married, realize that it takes work to maintain your love with God and a mate, too. It is a healthy desire to want to spend your life with a mate, but that is not a substitute for spending quality time loving God and yourself better.

Ecclesiastes 4:6 states that two is better than one, but, as Amos 3:3 says, how can two walk together except they be in agreement? You can even be unequally yoked to another person who says he or she is a Christian. A couple must be on one accord in order to have true relationship success. Plus, they need to be chosen and ordained by God.

Religious principles are a core value. II Corinthians 6:14 says to not be unequally yoked with unbelievers. A person saying that he or she is a Christian is not enough to ensure that the two of you are equally yoked. You need more than knowledge of God, but a personal relationship with Jesus Christ. Examine a person's attitudes and observe his or her actions to see whether or not he or she is actively walking out a faith-filled lifestyle. If he or she is not hungering and thirsting for righteousness and you are, keep stepping.

Bozo Or Boaz? *Don't Be Fooled By The Counterfeit.*

God plans to bring His divine mate into your life at His appointed time, but Satan's goal is to get you to miss your blessing. When a person nears the end of his or her single season, he or she must beware of tricks. The enemy always presents counterfeits before the real mate comes along. Like a fake one hundred dollar bill that can pass as a real one, counterfeits are finely camouflaged to look like real mates. They will have many attributes you are looking for, but always have a flaw that lets you know they are not it.

It's a common saying that if it looks like a duck, quacks like a duck and acts like a duck it probably is a duck. That is mostly true, but sometimes what looks like a duck from a distance is a finely crafted decoy. You have to closely and carefully examine your dates and prospective mates.

God knows what you like and so does the devil. Most counterfeits act like they love you, but they love benefits of being with you more. You imagine that their hearts are passionately for you, when usually they are not. "I want "to have my cake and eat it, too," is the counterfeit's creed.

Many times we settle for the counterfeit when the real prince or princess is at the next corner. Wasting too much time with the counterfeit can cause you to miss the real blessing, the person who God ordained to love you totally and completely with no motives or strings attached. As my mother taught me, "An ounce of prevention is worth a pound of cure." When you go beyond making a *good* choice and make a *godly* choice of your dates and mate, you can prevent a lot of future pain and the time it takes to cure it.

Women, Wait For God's Promise.

If you are not married yet, I encourage you to "wait for the promise." Do not stop short of the one God has for you. You can avoid the drama of being married and miserable when you do not rush into a relationship for the wrong reasons. I previously stated that married persons can feel painfully single when their spouses do not give them the security, attention, and appreciation they anticipated. That suffering can be eliminated when you wait for God's mate.

I have heard single women say that good men are hard to find. I have a question to ask about that perception, ladies. Why are you worried about finding the right man when he should be finding you? You never know what God is up to or who has been secretly checking you out. Isaac and Rebekah's story, told in Genesis 24, shows that God is all in the details of connecting a single woman to her ribcage. I Samuel 25's story of Abigail and the book of Ruth show how God prepared prosperous, godly husbands for widows. God will order your man's steps to you, too.

Someone sent me an email that said, "A woman's heart should be so close to God that a man has to seek God to find her." After all, a godly man will most likely be seeking a godly woman. So a single woman should serve the Lord with her whole heart and be the best woman she can so her mate can spot her in a crowd of women. By looking at all of her accomplishments, I believe the Proverbs 31 woman was excellent before marriage. When you are excellent in God, your future husband, too, will proclaim, "Many have done virtuously, but you excel them all." You will be praised!

Men, Let God Choose Your Mate.

Some single men say they are happy on their own and they mean it, but God placed the desire for true companionship in each one of us. Seasons change. At the appropriate time, your desire for marriage will increase to the point you know that your single days are almost over!

You don't have to be afraid of the institution of marriage. Some men hesitate because they fear failure. Some were traumatized by past marriage tragedy they witnessed or experienced. Others delay marriage because they are self-centered and irresponsible. Some do not think marriage is a necessary part of family life. Many persons live together for years and avoid the legal marriage commitment. They get many marriage benefits without the responsibility. Like me, you have probably heard people say, "Why buy the cow when you can get the milk for free?"

Other men love the institution of marriage and are not afraid to try because they want to be legal, which is respectable and responsible. However, many of these have found themselves in need of something more than a hookup. They need a holy hookup. They put themselves together for whatever reason, and now they still long to be connected with their God-ordained mates so they can have the maximum opportunity for marital fulfillment.

Prepare for your future bride now. Do not just seek the Lord for the woman of your dreams and not have anything to offer when you find her. Work while you wait. Invest and build your spiritual, emotional and financial success. God will bless your romantic relationship with success, too.

Singles And Sex

Have you had sex with a person you were not married to? If you have not, praise God. Wisely wait until marriage. But if you have, look back honestly and you will see that your relationship developed some issues after you acted outside of God's perfect plan. If you broke up after you were sexually involved, the pain was more severe than it would have been if you had not been intimate.

Without scripture, many people discredit what God has said, but with scripture, they can be convicted and change. So let me prove that God wants you to avoid sexual sins. I Thessalonians 4:3-4 makes it clear. It says, "For this is the will of God, even your sanctification, that you should abstain from fornication: that every one of you should know how to possess his vessel in sanctification and honor." I Corinthians 6:18 instructs us to flee fornication. That scripture's second sentence goes on to say that you sin against your own body when you commit fornication. Other scriptures that address sexual sin are Galatians 5:19, I Corinthians 6:13-18, II Corinthians 12:21, Ephesians 5:3, and Colossians 3:5. That should help you. Now if you are still wrestling with your flesh's feelings about this and what God's thoughts are about having sex outside of marriage, read I Corinthians 6:20. That scripture reminds you that you have been bought with a price; therefore, you should glorify God in your body and in your spirit which are God's. Your body is not your own. Jesus sacrificed His all for you. Are you sacrificing your self for Him? Oop there it is. Say "Amen" or repent and say "Ouch!"

God didn't tell us to flee fornication because He wanted to flex His ruler muscles and show off His Big Daddy status. No, God had Apostle Paul to write that wisdom to help His followers honor Him. God also wants to protect you physically, spiritually and emotionally.

Your date may persuade you to give in by saying that having sex is taking your relationship to a higher level, but don't believe that lie. Sex has the opposite effect when you are single. Having sex prematurely does not help develop your relationship. It actually hinders it. Like an animal in heat, your focus goes to having more sex. You don't have as many long conversations to find out what you really need to know about him or her because your craving flesh can't wait to get between the sheets again.

Singles can get strung out on sex's highly addictive fleshy pleasure and lose fellowship with God! God is not against sex, but He is against you having sex outside of marriage. He created sex to be exclusively enjoyed between husbands and wives. Marriage is the only union big and strong enough to hold lovemaking's powerful emotions.

Marriage may be in your future, but doing the right thing at the wrong time is the wrong thing to do. Disobeying God to please the flesh does not bring His blessing or make someone love you. Boldly disobeying God and having unmarried sex repeatedly still does not guarantee you true love from the person you slept with. It hurts severely to have your pearls trampled over by swine. You must pay *before* you ride a bus, train or plane. Singles, don't let anyone ride *you* without paying first! Understand?

Wisdom For The Single And Seeking

God really ministered to me as a single woman and He kept me out of a lot of trouble. One time I thought I was doing very well because God had kept me sexually pure, but my ego started to get a little bit inflated. The Lord spoke to me and stuck a pin in my balloon. He let me know that I was able to accomplish sexual purity not because I was so good, had my head on right and took delight in His word. Oh no. He reminded me that I was still walking around in a flesh suit daily. I was as susceptible as anyone to sin, so I could not possibly keep myself! He reminded me that I was standing not because of my good works, but because He kept me pure and kept much temptation away.

As Christians, we may not be of this world, but we still live in the world. I want to pour out practical wisdom that coincides with the spiritual truths God taught me while waiting for my God-ordained dream mate. He taught me that singles should be moving targets in hot pursuit of life. Ladies, how can your king chase you when you are sitting still? Do not sit around waiting for someone to come along and make you happy. You will not have a happy future relationship when one or both persons are emotionally unhappy and not in perfect peace. Get to know yourself. Become a happy individual. Marriage can't do that for you.

When you think you are ready, make sure you date for the right reasons--not to be popular or make others jealous. Be careful of rebound relationships or dating someone who has a particular attribute of a love you once had and lost. When the illusion fades, you will have heartache, not joy.

Ask your date what his or her goal is for dating you. If he or she does not have an immediate answer, allow time to think about it because you want it to come from the heart. Be sure to discuss this early and again later down the road. If he or she puts it off, pay attention. If something is said that you were not expecting, do not ignore it. Listen!

If you date persons dealing with drama, you will not be able to have a drama-free relationship with them. Pray, but give time and space for them to get their lives in order on their own. It won't take many dates before you get dragged down into their confusion. Release them to God and trust Him. He can keep everything that is committed to Him. God will bring you back together in His appointed time *if* your relationship is predestined by Him.

Here is some additional wisdom to remember.

- ♥ You cannot make anyone truly love you.
- ♥ You won't marry a punk if you don't date one.
- ♥ Be careful how you treat others. Remember that you will reap what you sow.
- ♥ Ladies don't be desperate. Men sense neediness.
- ♥ Leave involved persons alone. You are good enough to be the object of one person's affection.
- ♥ Wake up. The fact that a person is in the church does not mean that Christ is living in him or her.
- ♥ Having a baby does not hold a bad relationship together or make a man or woman commit.
- ♥ Ladies, do not think he is going to marry or respect you if you keep giving him sex freely.

The Spiritual Attraction Factor

God blessed me with a revelation about spiritual attraction that I believe will truly bless you. I was taught that men and women are three part beings; spirit, soul and body. The body is a shell. The soul contains our emotions, will and mind and the spirit is the part of us closest to God.

Love is very emotional and falling in love is wonderful. *Soul mate* is a common term that reflects when two people feel like they have found the person they will love forever. They feel like they are one accord then. But don't you know celebrities and everyday people who said they had met their soul mates; however, their relationships did not last?

I believe you know now that God has a specific preordained mate for you and a joint spiritual purpose for the two of you. God desires for us to experience spiritual love. Therefore, I have coined the term *Spirit mate*™.

Adam and Eve were *Spirit mates*. He recognized his wife because she came from him. Like Adam, God's men should be attracted to a person who they see themselves in. Men are supposed to recognize her similar spirit, claim her and loudly say, "This is bone of my bone and flesh of my flesh!"

Your *Spirit mate* is more than a soul mate could ever be. You worship the same God the same way and have the same love and willingness to sacrifice self to please Him. When God brings you together, your spiritual and natural love is strong, sizzling and undeniable. All must recognize God's pre-ordained mate, your destiny connected marriage partner which He had in mind before He formed you in the womb. Your *Spirit mate* is God's gift. Do not settle for less.

ACT III

Discovering Your Dream

CHAPTER EIGHT

Love And Sports

Strategies for Relationship Success

Drama-free relationships are the result of a successful team effort.
- Lynetta Jordan

Relationships are partnerships and love is a team sport. All team sports are joint efforts which require the cooperation and collaboration of all team members to be a total success. Championships can only be won when team players are unified and work together in harmony to achieve the same goal. One teammate can disqualify the entire team if he or she selfishly tries to play the game alone. Some victories have to be shared. And so it is in love.

It takes two to make a relationship work; however, you probably know one person who tries to take all the credit for success. It's just like when an athlete attempts to steal the show on camera and take all the credit for the team's victory. One person may score the game's winning points, but he or she should never forget that it was a team win. If the teammates had not blocked the opposition, scoring would not have been possible. Couples can score in love when they follow the same game plan and work in unison. It takes both to make a successful relationship team.

A Team Fighting Internally Cannot Win Any Game.

Constructive communication is a critical key to every relationship's success. Without it, it will be impossible to have *love without the drama*. Every couple will face some type of minor or major conflict, so they must learn to discuss and resolve their problems respectfully, without screaming and conniving. The couple should discuss, pray, consider both of their points of view and seek counsel if needed until they reach a consensus, which is even better than a compromise. Though consensus is not always reached quickly, it ensures that both loves are listened to and agree to move forward together in one clear direction.

Keep conflict confidential. Disagreements should be handled between each other in the privacy of your home, so do not take your conflict out in the streets. Some couples carry their business to the streets too fast, but the Bible advises us to handle conflicts directly with a brother or sister first. If that brother or sister does not listen, we are still not to tell the whole neighborhood! Openly exposing private conflict to the public can dismantle a team and give its enemies and opponents a huge advantage over them.

Teammates are expected to handle their "locker room" conflicts in the privacy of the locker room. Owners, coaches and associations require players to consider the team sport as a higher call than their individual interests, so severe penalties are enforced when they display disunity publicly. When they go out and play the game, they are expected to put differences aside and be inseparable. Though conflict still needs resolution, opponents should not detect it.

As teammates, you are in it to win at love together. When you are on the right team, the presence of conflict does not mean that you get frustrated, walk off and stop playing. Focusing on team spirit will remind you that you are not opponents, but friends and help you to work it out.

Romans 12:18 instructs that as much as it is possible, live peaceably with all men. Sometimes peace is not possible until a problem is confronted. Disagreements can make you question a relationship's stability, but differing opinions do not mean that it is over. When you love peace like I do, tense moments can scare you a bit, but I have learned that it is better to let out that steam often than have bottled frustration explode inside you until you scream for relief. Very few problems get resolved in screaming matches.

A disrespectful tone of voice will cause a personal foul. After calm, but difficult discussions when I expressed my feelings as lovingly as I could, I asked the Lord to deal with him directly and show him plainly what I was saying and how heartfelt my love still was. Not only did God minister to him, but He reassured me that all was well, too!

Couples should deal with conflict with lovingkindness. As challenging as it may seem, it is possible. You should not confront each other with fists or a worse weapon, a sharp insulting tongue. It amazes me how many couples are still together, yet disrespect each other face to face and talk bad about each other to other people. When you put down your mate publicly, you are putting yourself down, too. Don't be found guilty of running his or her name in the mud because some of that mud will splash back on you!

External Conflict

The devil roams about as a roaring lion seeking whom he may devour, so don't let him devour your relationship. Kingdom couples must be on alert and defense against lies the enemy spreads through haters with hopes to distract, divide and ultimately destroy their God-ordained team.

Every prospective date or mate does not intend to play love games, but outsiders who play games will falsely accuse you of playing games, too. Though your lover truly intends to love you with no strings attached, haters will make accusations that their true love is just a gimmick. So be on guard for external conflict sent from the pits of hell.

You must use what you have learned about your lover in private to fight the temptation to believe lies the enemy tells publicly that sound similar to truth. I Thessalonians 5:12 advises to know them that labor among you, so spend quality time in conversations, public and private fellowship to get to know your teammate thoroughly, deeply and by the spirit. Carnally minded haters portray people by flesh. You should trust and know your love more intimately than any accuser. Learn to discern his or her heart. Do not be so easily swayed by deceptive tactics and false perceptions from the mouth of love's enemies. Ultimately, you should know his or her character best, so defend it before liars.

I take kingdom relationships very seriously. Behind the scenes, I had former friends with envy issues fall out of fellowship with me like Lucipher fell from heaven. Masked as genuinely interested friends, these inquisitive (NOSY!) folks dug for details of my life, ministry and business.

These two-faced, double-minded associates were devils disguised as angels of light right in my social circle! They leaked relationship success stories to camouflaged enemies who wore friend masks, then listened to their derogatory, discrediting remarks without defending me. Some misused their past association with me to deceive present friends. They misrepresented me and my true motives. They said I said things that I never did say. They tried to undermine me by taking pieces of facts, adding their "two cents worth" to that and deceptively presenting their version as the whole truth. Since these persons appeared to have been close associates, it made their stories even more believable.

I was crushed when people considered what disguised angels of light said about me as truth without giving me an opportunity to speak for myself. You must remember that the devil intensifies attacks against all that is of God that he knows will tear his kingdom down. That crafty rascal tells lies and makes them seem true, then twists the truth to create believable lies. We are in a war. As you mature in Christ, you should despise gossip and get to its root, too.

Take it from me, do not believe or act on rumors without facing your date or mate to truly listen to his or her side first. Even when the gossip seems like it may have some truth, confront your love directly before you think about considering the accusations of rumorbearers. Do not shun, avoid or refuse to listen to your love. I was unaware of weapons formed against me, but if I had been confronted first and sincerely listened to, I could have intervened before my haters' dramatic plots and schemes did damage.

I like to get to the root of a problem so I can save time by solving it, but I have learned that gossipers do not like to be confronted to expose the truth. When I wanted to confront the root of a rumor, the gossip's carrier refused to disclose the source. That really angered me because I was on my way to confronting the source because gossip wastes times and ruins lives. How many grudges could have been released and misjudgments dismissed if people only confronted those the enemy accused of being culprits first?

Since love is a team sport, we must take attacks against our teammates seriously and defend them from malicious, demonic conspiracies against God-ordained relationships. Because Luke 10:19 declares that God has given me power to tread upon serpents and scorpions and all the works of the enemy, I have launched a vicious counterattack on the enemies of love. Since the weapons of my warfare are not carnal but mighty through God to the pulling down of strongholds, I will use every key to the kingdom Jesus gave me. Join me in fighting and prevailing through prayer, praise, worship, fasting, binding, loosing and speaking to every mountain that needs to move out of the way of love. Kingdom relationships are serious, so I am taking back everything the enemy stole from me. I want his spoils, too!

Where there is unity there is strength. A unified relationship, especially a marriage, is a continual threat to Satan. That's why we must recognize that he will appear as an angel of light to try to dismantle the Lord's doing. His weapons against me will not work any longer. I'm paying him back by empowering other kingdom relationships, too.

Love And Sports

In every sport, players must train regularly to keep their muscles strong and intact. If they cease to exercise, they may be short-winded or experience other difficulties when it is time to play and go for the win. As your personal trainer, I am impressed at your workout so far. You have gained a new understanding of properly handling internal and external relationship conflict. Now that I believe you know how much love is like a team sport, you can wipe your sweat. As you cool down, relax your muscles with these light-hearted relationship success strategies.

Love Is Like Boxing: You can lose a round and still win the fight if you stay in the ring and don't get knocked out.

Love Is Like Tennis: Someone has to be the first to serve.

Love Is Like Bowling: Just in case you did not bowl a strike the first time, thank the Lord for a second chance.

Love Is Like Synchronized Swimming: You must be on one accord to win and when you are, it will be beautiful.

Love Is Like A Team Relay. You cannot win it by yourself. It takes everyone's best individual efforts for the team to win. Though you pass the baton to your teammate, you must stay in position in case you have to run again.

Love Is Like Gymnastics: If you fall, just get back up.

Love Is Like The Shotput: You can't hold on to heavy, burdensome weight. You must cast your cares far to win.

Love Is Like Volleyball: Sometimes your positions rotate. This is not just about sex, it is about life. Volleyball is exciting because everyone gets a turn to serve and support. You don't stay in the same position for the whole game. Couples may have to take turns encouraging one another.

Love Is Like Basketball: You may have the ball now, but be humble enough to know that your opponent can get the rebound. Having the ball in your hands is a great opportunity for you to score, but arrogance can cause you to miss the perfect shot. Queen Vashti's story in the book of Esther demonstrates that an "it's all about me" attitude can disqualify you and have you taken out of the game.

Love Is Like Football: You can only make a touchdown when your teammate blocks the enemy. But don't ignore the referee's penalty flags that can cancel a winning play.

Love Is Like Baseball: With focus you can hit a home run.

Love Is Like Golf: With great skill, concentration and effort you can make a hole in one.

Love Is Like Soccer: You must learn how to kick the ball beyond the adversary who is trying to block your success.

CHAPTER NINE

Security Matters

The Importance of Protecting Your Relationship

Protect what you value. Drama-free relationships are priceless.
- Lynetta Jordan

A painful personal experience taught me the importance of protecting your relationship's privacy. The enemy of our souls specializes in sending serpents and spies to interfere with the harmony and unity of God-ordained relationships. Evil interference can cause a couple indescribable heartache and excruciating headache. Deception and delusion can delay divine blessings, postpone a proposal and cut off communication. Busybody's rumors, gossip and lies have triggered far too much distrust, division and divorce.

"Haters" take off their masks when you fall in love for real! I hate to break the news, but all in your circle may not be truly happy for you. They fall into one of two categories: *haters* or *celebrators*. If persons you believe to be *celebrators* have even one percent of envy, jealousy, anger, resentment or evil wishes toward you, they are qualified *haters*. Haters cannot be trusted to treasure the prized possession of your true love story. They will negatively expose, destroy or try to twist your dream and turn it into drama every time.

Protecting your relationship is a serious security matter. I'm not trying to make you suspicious of everyone, but I am advising you as the Bible says, to watch as well as pray. Many people know the language and talk the right talk, but they are not all walking the true walk of sincere friendship. If I can help you avoid the pain and destiny delays I have experienced because of what I did not know at first, this chapter is well worth my journey. My pain was not in vain.

It is true that you will reap what you sow, good or bad. I found out that your good reaping may not always come from the people you sowed good into. Because I was truly happy for the success of others, I assumed they would be genuinely happy for me, too, especially since I had never done or said anything to harm them and supported them and their families in good and bad times. I didn't criticize their crazy actions, but respected their relationship choices and encouraged them along life's way. Yet, they could not support my success. In fact, some tried to destroy my love.

You are probably familiar with the adage, "Misery loves company." I painfully discovered its truth years ago. My love glow and beaming rays of happiness revealed others' darkness. Friends' camouflaged misery became exposed!

It is amazing who claims to be your friend until you seem to get one step ahead of them and they try to trip you. Like crabs in a bucket, when you appear to reach freedom, another will claw you to pull you back down into the low place. I'm still waiting to understand all the reasons why, but sadly it seems that sometimes those who should be the happiest for you struggle with your love success the most.

The Bible advises us to be wise as serpents and harmless as doves. Wisdom and experience have taught me to limit what relationship details I disclose to certain friends and family in order to avoid intrusion of the enemy into my love life. I naively assumed that the hearts of some past friends were as genuine, loving and harmless as mine, but later found they were not. They were undercover "haters."

Cleverly disguised as friends, some of these haters wore tight masks. They accompanied to me to events and intently listened to my God-given revelations, visions, dreams and ideas. Most of us had even prayed, praised and worshipped the Lord together. But a few of these "sisters," disguised as angels of light, had impure motives and stony hearts. Some possessed secret envy and were jealous, angry and insecure. Though they hid their dysfunctions well, some had miserable private lives. God and life taught me that when some person's lives are out of control, they may seek personal validation by attempting to control yours.

While I had chosen to wait to marry God's true ordained mate, some people around me were impatient, had settled and were angry about results of choices they made on their own. Jealous and treacherous, some tried to sabotage my success. One sister talked and acted like she had her romance together. By her initial reaction, I thought she was excited with me about my new found friend--especially since she was quick to encourage me in a past dead-end relationship. Unfortunately, I discovered too late that she was sowing discord, causing confusion and disruption. She smiled in my face, but she was stabbing me in my back.

The pain of betrayal of friends and family did not begin today. King David experienced it in Biblical times. He expressed his woe in Psalms 55:12-14. In summary, he said that if it was a known *enemy* that had reproached him he could have borne it. But what hurt him most was that it was his familiar friend and equal, one who he had sweet fellowship with. They had even worshipped God together. Who told you that the Bible is not relevant to everyday life?

Known and unknown haters exist in your outer circle, but you may have a few in your inner circle, too. They do not always appear as opponents. Hater traits can show up in family members, coworkers, friends, fraternity, sorority, social and unfortunately, even religious group members.

You must watch as well as pray about people around you. If you see a snake and veer off its path, you can avoid its dangerous bite. Be aware of nosy busybodies and crafty individuals who engage in smooth conversation, but aim to inject poisonous influence, find fault or information to use against you. If they gossip about others to you, you're next.

Learning the traits of haters helps prevent pain they could cause you. Detection is not always instant. Haters must be discerned because their deception lies within. Their filthy hearts are overshadowed by clean outward appearances. Haters can include your "garbage can friends" who collect gossip, whose lives are full of junk and who dump problems on you but never change. They may despise you when you are truly happy and your love life is clutter free. These destiny stealers will expose confidential conversations to drag you into their mud of misery. Oh no!

Now, my friend, let's make this even more personal. Examine yourself and look into the mirror of your life. Perhaps *you* have been the one who has hated on others in the past. Maybe you felt life had dealt you an unfair hand or you had made bad choices and were upset with people who seemed to "have it made." Hurting people hurt other people. If you were hurting and not yet healed, bitter and not yet better, there is a good chance you were a hater. When your heart bleeds you can choose to get a bandage or wound someone else to make them feel pain, too. If in the past you chose to make an uninvolved party bleed, you were a hater. Those actions may be why you have continued to experience relationship misery in the present.

Speaking of the present, are you hating on a friend, family member, or co-laborer? People with jealous spirits can even be envious of people they do not personally know. Jealous hearts aim to destroy and kill anything joyfully alive. When you have been viciously attacked by it like I have, you will know beyond a shadow of a doubt that as Song of Solomon 8:6 says, jealousy is cruel as the grave.

Examine yourself. When you are not healed from past hurt, it is easy to become a hater. If words of disbelief fly out your mouth when you hear of someone's happiness or you suddenly get a negative attitude of doubt and discredit another's sincerity, you just might be a hater. If you act as if you are happy for people when the truth is that you are not, you just might be a hater. If you pretend to be a friend while hoping to find fault in someone's personal life to use against him or her later, you are definitely a hater.

God's displeasure with certain "gamelike" behaviors is a great reason to leave misery and bitterness behind. Proverbs 6:16-19 confirms that God hates the wicked deeds of haters and lists seven traits and deeds many miserable and bitter people participate in. Don't overlook these, because one of them may apply to you! The attitudes and actions the Lord despises are: a proud look, a lying tongue, hands that shed innocent blood, a heart that devises wicked thoughts and plans, feet that are swift in running to mischief, a false witness that speaks lies, and someone who sows discord among brethren. It adds, the Lord *hates* these things. In fact, the seventh is an abomination to Him.

The immature behavior of trying to demolish someone else's relationship dream castle can cause you to anger and upset God. It infuriates Him when you undermine His children with those deeds He hates. You don't want to get on His bad side because He is still a God of wrath who repays evil. He is also a God of justice who will execute vengeance when you hurt people who have not harmed you. So if you do not change soon, you will suffer more as you will continually reap of the bad seeds you have sown.

The truth may hurt, but I must tell you the truth in love. Haters should not expect to have *love without the drama*. If you are involved in acts of hatred rather than celebration, you will reap the discord and division you are sowing. If you are deceptive, malicious, backbiting, jealous and practice evil works, you will hurt yourself much more than the person you aim to injure with your insinuations, words, thoughts and deeds. Please stop drinking that Hatorade!

As I reflected on past pain I suffered from the deeds of haters, a present friend and prayer warrior opened my eyes. She pointed out that every one of the persons who sought to hinder my relationship and marriage is either not currently married or not part of a godly, healthy and flourishing relationship. They may flounce around and talk as if they are completely satisfied with life, but in reality they are suffering. Some even talk negatively about others thinking that they will make themselves look or feel better.

Those persons' actions caused me tremendous pain, but I did not have to wish harm on them. Some people think they can run over you when you don't fight back with fists, but not so. I humble myself and let God fight my battles. He takes care of all vengeance for me and His payback is greater than mine. It has taken maturity to realize that I can't physically injure anyone equivalent to the emotional pain I felt. Besides, *two wrongs still do not add up to one right.*

Thanks to the love, grace, mercy and forgiveness of God, you do not have to stay in the misery of your past. You do not have to remain a hater and continue to reap the fruit that grows when you sow evil and supplant others. Why should you want to live like that when God's way is better?

You can repent to God, ask forgiveness of those you offended and convert from *hater* to *celebrator*. Celebrators' hearts are free and not weighted with hatred, envy or jealousy. They confidently live in an overflow of God's joy, peace and security, knowing that celebrating with others does not subtract any attention from them. Life is happier for celebrators. Do you want to be one? I knew you would!

Beware Of Dream Killers And Destiny Stealers.

I'll be the first person to admit that it is hard to keep true love to yourself. You absolutely cannot hide it. When you fall in love hard, love radiates through almost everything you do. Your conversation, body language and actions reflect it. You feel bubbly inside. There's a sparkle in your eyes, a skip in your step and an extra wide smile every time you think of your beloved. Your heart turns cartwheels for a love song like *Always and Forever* or *When I'm With You*.

You feel so good that you want to share the highlights of your romantic rendezvous, long conversations, romantic dinners, walks in the park and surprises that made your heart flutter down to the details. You find it hard not to share with friends your wonderful experience with this caring person who makes you happier than ever. But beware of disclosing the details. When true love is overflowing from your heart, you need to be very selective of who you share even a tidbit of your joy-filled love stories with. Why? Because everyone is not happy for you. You may encounter the dream killers and destiny stealers at your happiest moment! Their faces may truly surprise you.

I have known spiritually sick, selfish people who tried to sabotage others' joyful relationships. It was unbelievably tough when I learned that some people you have faithfully celebrated with and supported wholeheartedly will fail to celebrate with you. You, too, may be the kind of person who celebrates the success of others and who would never discourage or damage another's relationship; however, everyone around you does not have jealousy under control.

My friend, it can be dangerous to share your love's joy too freely with some people! II Corinthians 11:14 says that even Satan himself can disguise himself as an angel of light. I have seen that gleam in the eye and heard the curiosity in the voices of those Satan was trying to use to interfere with my present and trace my future. He will use anyone he can!

I was unaware of some of the enemy's sneaky tricks. I recall one "friend" who turned out to be desperately jealous and envious. I had known her, or at least thought I knew her, for years. I trusted this woman who said she served the Lord and who boasted like she had a wonderful love life. She was older and I assumed that experience had made her wiser. I believed she would offer confidential godly, mature and womanly wisdom as I was considering possibly furthering a new friendship. But this woman who should have been a mentor actually became a meddler.

I was extremely excited about this new male friend God sent my way at the perfect time in my life. The opposite of my past dead-end friend, this man and I had an amazing spiritual connection. We were unified in our effervescent love for the Lord, shared the same extravagant relationship dreams and both loved to worship, laugh and have fun!

My former sister-friend who should have been happy for me, envied my glow. Like Sherlock Holmes, she interrogated me to dig for any details she could get. Later, she let the enemy use her to try to ruin us. As deceivers, gossipers, and slanderers do, she stabbed me in my back and twisted the truth. Her envious actions caused serious hurt, confusion and misunderstanding between him and I.

It was a security tragedy. The initial blow traumatized me severely and my wounded heart bled for days, weeks and months to come. The grief was greater than I had ever experienced with anyone living or dead. But because I let go and let God handle the vengeance, I'm sure the harvest she reaped from what she had sowed was ten times worse.

Her jealousy was murderous. I felt jealousy's sting and saw how it was cruel as the grave. Only an unredeemed, twisted mind could be proud of causing anybody pain like that. It seemed she was aiming to sabotage and destroy me, someone I deeply cared for and our positive, healthy new friendship. Perhaps she envied and resented my genuine joy of a healthy relationship built on God's principles arriving in my life after I had experienced the opposite, but isn't that when true friends are supposed to be happy for you? Though she never apologized to me, I released her to God so I could be free and my bleeding heart could heal.

This drama-filled sister wore her happy mask tightly. Mind you, my guard was not up because we fellowshipped in Christian circles. Weeks before her back-stabbing came to light, I felt spiritually sick and dismal. My friend nor I understood it. I did not know what was happening then, but my spirit felt Satan's plot in progress. Fortunately, God spoke directly to me hours before her evil deeds and the words of those who carried her tales were exposed. When I opened my Bible at the waterfront, God gave me three scriptures to stand on. One of them was Isaiah 54:17, which declares that no weapon formed against me shall prosper. Ultimately, the enemy's wicked plans did not prevail.

Keep Your Business Private.

It is sad to say, but some people you consider friends or family cannot protect the personal business you may want to share. Everyone cannot handle the details you reveal of your success and personal failures. You must watch out for gleaming eyes and smooth moves from some of your close associates. When you get an itch to talk, try some of these things. Write it in a private journal, talk to God about it or talk to a teddy bear and make sure no one else is at home!

When your love is not properly protected by you, it is open to the enemy's attack. Understand this. The serpent's deception in the garden of Eden was foreshadowing for other God-ordained relationships. Adam and Eve had destiny attached to their love. The enemy only attacks the best, that is, God-ordained relationships, because they are his greatest threat. God-ordained love can change a nation.

Keeping your business private minimizes the drama of negative outside influences penetrating your relationship. Deceitful people who I was a faithful friend to tried to influence others against loving me. A person you admire and love dearly may have tried to turn you against the very person God sent to love you. They often offer unsolicited opinions, certain insinuations, comments and suggestions to cause doubt, distrust and discord that can ruin your relationship. When you hear "If I were you…," remember they are not. It is *your* life. Take time to pray, listen to God's voice and do what He says, not them. Stop being led by their attitudes and opinions. Don't let them stop you from pursuing your love dreams that God ordained to manifest.

Qualify Your Confidants.

All counsel, even from persons with the counselor title, is not wise. (Why is it that some people who try to offer the most advice are ones who know the least?) God usually sends you one or two true friends you can confide in who will not judge, but minister to you. You won't have many!

Proverbs 13:20 says, "He who walks with wise men shall himself be wise, but with a companion of fools shall be destroyed." You need to know those who labor among you. When someone offers advice, dig deeper to discover their wisdom and true motives. From experience I know that motives can be hidden well. Sneaky people will draw close and camouflage their true intentions to try to get you to divulge personal information. After they think they have found a flaw or obtained something juicy about you, they dash to take it back to the enemy's camp. Some will break ties or stop calling if they are unsuccessful and you do not disclose gossip-worthy information within a certain time.

You should also observe your confidant's histories to see if they are living the lives they talk about. It's surprising how many childish thinkers and actors are walking around in adult bodies. You can be shocked by the actions of immature or insecure adult friends and family who do not like it when someone new enters your life. Unbeknownst to you, some have taken advantage of your time to push their own agendas and live through you. Some fear your new love will take the time or money they got from you. It may startle you who gets upset when you have a prosperous relationship. It could even be those you considered close.

Many people like to keep you close in view so they can keep a watch on your progress. I recall Pastor Paula White preaching that you challenge others when you step out of the boat. Those left inside have to justify why they are still there, so they try to pull you back in. They don't want you to get ahead first. That's jealousy, envy and covetousness, too. God has enough for us all, so we have no reason to envy others. I'm glad that what God has for me is for me.

God has designed it so that people are in your life for either a reason, a season or a lifetime. So if a friend gets mad at you and starts acting funny, let that childish adult go. Bishop T.D. Jakes calls it having the gift of goodbye. When you wise up, people get mad when they can no longer manipulate, use and influence you the way they used to. Some offered their opinions rather than God's word as advice. I have known some to use scripture, but twist its context. Allowing even one outside person to wrongly influence you or your perception of your love can be dangerous. The miserable will rob you of your destiny.

When you are a dreamer, your big vision exposes small thinking. It is small minds who talk about people. Average minds talk about events. Great minds talk about ideas. If you have "friends" who talk about others, at some point they will gossip and maybe even lie about you. It never fails. We excuse gossip because of the people who tell it, but it is what it is. Hang around garbage cans (gossipers) and you will eventually smell trash, smell like trash or get it on you! Make God your best friend. He won't tell your business, spread rumors or lies. He keeps His mouth shut!

You may feel it helps you to share your situations with a physical person to help you make right decisions. Talking it out does help you feel listened to, but here is something else you need to think through. You can't tell most friends or family what you don't want repeated to another person. Like a bottomless bucket, some people can't hold anything!

Tell it all to the Lord. If you have a rough relationship moment and tell all your business to the wrong persons, they will never forget it. People will hold grudges against your date or mate long after the two of you make up and progress past rough moments. When it appears you are moving forward and making progress in the relationship, those you told can use this as a weapon to hinder you. Though your darling has done 100 things right since then, some confidants will intermingle your past and present and constantly remind you of what he or she did then. This kind of interference has triggered many divorces. Beware!

In the counsel of the wise there is safety, but you must closely watch and pray to properly discern whether or not a person is wise counsel. Everyone who has been in a similar situation does not qualify as wise counsel either. For example, a person who has been married before does not automatically qualify to counsel yours. Some marriages had quantity of time but no quality of life, so don't base a couple's wisdom on their number of years together. Just because they stayed a long time does not mean it was God's will or handled God's way. On the contrary, God can use someone who has not been married to speak life into your marriage, so don't discredit or disqualify them either.

God anointed and empowered me as a single woman to minister His wisdom and word to transform and improve marriages. Some people said to themselves that I could not tell them anything about marriage when I was not married. Their first thoughts were natural, carnal, but those who were spiritual soon acknowledged the word of the Lord on my lips. When couples listened and applied the Bible-based, practical wisdom He spoke through me on radio, in seminars and conferences, their relationships improved.

Do not miss God's voice of wisdom when it does not come from the person or source you think. There are times when a person who is not in your situation or never has been can offer you appropriate Bible-based wisdom. So don't disqualify a message because of its messenger as long as it is truth. If He used a donkey to speak to Balaam in Numbers 22, you know He can use people to speak to you.

I hosted a women's conference in September 2007. The theme, "It's The Ninth Month And You Are Due For Your Breakthrough," was a spiritual metaphor to encourage women to give birth to God's destiny inside of them. After the invited speakers ministered on conception and the first, second and third trimesters, I concluded with "Labor and Delivery." I had no children, so some debated how I could deliver that topic. Dressed in a white labcoat like a doctor, I came out preaching with fire. I dispelled doubt when I asked, "How do you trust a male doctor to deliver your baby when he has never had one?" The answer is, you trust a person who has not been where you are when he or she has the knowledge, education, training or gift to help you.

Even In Your Excitement, You Must Protect Your Dream.

Love sent from God can and will be absolutely exciting! He designed it that way. Yet, I cannot emphasize enough how much happy couples need to know the importance of protecting their relationships from unqualified opinions of outside influences--dream killers and destiny stealers.

I'm telling you, it can be very hard to discern who is happy now and will remain happy for you. I shared how hurt I was when a person I had been a genuine friend and blessing to, supported and had committed no crime against attempted to destroy me and my new friendship with her poisonous, gossiping lips. As all two-faced persons do, it's possible that she was talking about me behind my back before I began to walk through the door to my dream, but I only saw the smile on her face, not the knife in her hand. Like the perfect actress, she still acted as if she was a friend. I am a 100% friend, so I accepted her actions as her decision to be my enemy and discard our friendship for no logical reason. I tearfully thanked God for uncovering her true character before she caused more disruption in my life. But still, the formed weapon's impact on my new friendship hurt me in a way I would never want anyone else to suffer.

What the enemy intended for evil toward me, God has worked for my good. Our great and mighty God honors His word and gets all the glory. In His sovereignty He knew my suffering then would minister to, heal and prepare people worldwide now. He brought me through with victory to lead you to experience victory. I thank God for the good, but I do not want to repeat that episode again.

Minimizing the opposition and warfare against God-ordained relationships has become extremely important to me. The people you think will be the happiest may not be. In the Old Testament, Joseph discovered how close haters can be. He was so excited about the dream God gave him; however, his own family tried to kill him after he shared it. It happens. My biological family was glad for me, but some of my spiritual "family" actually prayed and spoke against the true blessing God prepared for me. That is witchcraft!

Spiritual and natural warfare are not new. When the enemy gets a glimpse of the next blessing God is sending to you, it seems all hell breaks loose. Though he can't snatch the blessing, the enemy's goal is to get you to give up before you receive it. In Daniel 10, it took twenty one days, three weeks, for Daniel's answer to prayer to arrive. The angel explained that God heard him when he first prayed, but the answer was delayed because the prince of Persia withstood him. That was intense spiritual warfare.

Sharing love's details makes it easy for the enemy and those he uses to trace your relationship. Masked friends who are envious, critical, insecure or busybodies meddling in other's affairs often let the enemy use them. They will cheerfully help you miss your blessing as they try to drown out God's voice with their sweet talk and strong opinions.

Don't let everyone in your business. Consider controlling privacy settings on social networking sites. You cannot always respond affirmatively to every friend request either. Although the screen may say "add a friend," everyone is not a friend to you or your relationship. Some are just nosy!

Hurting People Hurt Other People.

Misery loves company. You may have a family member, co-worker or neighbor who is living a miserable life right now. Some are easy to recognize. They open their mouths and negativity pours out. If you were feeling fine, you may be on the verge of depression by the time you finish listening to their pessimistic conversation. But some people skillfully camouflage their misery beneath beaming stories of how well their children are doing, how much they have and how happy they are. Some will even offer their advice for your life decisions. Their misery is hard to trace because they talk a good game and may deceptively seem as if they have an answer to every question in the world. Inside they are battling self-esteem issues, competing with others and fighting to maintain their own mental stability.

Some "miserable" people are emotionally unbalanced. They want to be the center of attention and get extremely upset when they see others smile or hear their lively stories of life endeavors that are going well. It is terrible that some dissatisfied adults who are regretful about their own lives childishly and foolishly try to demolish the joy of others. You build your dream castle in the sand and they will kick it down before the high tide. They thrive on mischief and will punish other genuinely happy people who are living in peace and harmony with themselves and others.

You should never want to be in the state that you are so dissatisfied with your own life that you try to hurt someone else in any way. If this is you, confess, change your mind and your ways today. Don't hate. Celebrate!

External Drama. *The influence of slithering serpents.*

Outside influence affected the original relationship. Adam and Eve started in the perfect state, a perfect man and woman ready to walk out their purposes. But what happened along the way? They listened to the wrong voice.

Even though Adam and Eve were the first and only people on earth at the time, the serpent that God created interfered with and disrupted their perfect union. The woman listened to the serpent, influenced her husband and they both ate the fruit. By yielding to bad outside influence, they messed up their harmonious relationship with God and contaminated their perfect union. You may have yielded to serpent-like friends and family's influence, too.

Disobedience led to mankind being cursed and perfect relationships broken. Thanks be to God, He did not leave man in that miserable state. Jesus Christ was God's plan to redeem mankind from the consequences of Adam and Eve's fall. The thief came to steal, kill and destroy in the garden and he is still on that mission. But Jesus, our Savior, came that we might have life and life more abundantly.

If your relationship has been hurt by a security breach, even if it was your fault, I have great news. You can recover. God had a master plan to redeem Adam and Eve from the curses they brought upon themselves after heeding the suggestions of an ungodly outside influence. He has a master plan to restore you, too. In fact, Joel 2:25 says that God will restore to you the years the locust, cankerworm, caterpillar and the palmerworm have eaten. My friend, God will redeem the time just for you.

Love covers a multitude of sins, including loose lips. I do not want you to repeat the security mistakes of your past. To prevent damage in your future, study to be quiet. You cannot tell some people, even some family and friends, stories about your relationship success. I know it is hard to believe, but everyone is just not happy for you. Thank God for those who follow Romans 12:15, "Rejoice with those who rejoice and weep with those who weep," and do truly celebrate your success. However, everyone doesn't do that.

Losing someone valuable who cannot easily be replaced can make you feel so sad and heartbroken. Protect your relationship as if it were a priceless, rare, special cut jewel needing top security at all times. Do not let busybodies in your business or your home because they may be snooping around to find a way to break in, disrupt and steal your treasured love and harmony. It's terrible to think that some people do that, but it is the truth. Welcome blessings, but do not feel obligated to answer the door for surprise visits from meddling friends and relatives. Some persons, even parents, who do not have happy lives can try to control and relive their lives through you. A courtesy call never hurt anyone, so it will not hurt them to respect and call you.

Security is a serious matter. Protect the beautiful love God prepared and sent especially to you. Fight for God's promise and do not let anyone separate you from your God-ordained love. Some will celebrate, but some may hate, so watch as well as pray when you share your love dreams. Do not forget the wisdom I gained from my pain. *You never know who is miserable until you are truly happy.*

CHAPTER TEN
Love Without The Drama
Why Settle When Relationships Can Sizzle?

Getting to real love without the drama can be a journey. Lust will not last, but real love will be worth every mile of the trip. – Lynetta Jordan

Is your present relationship *sizzling* or *fizzling*? _____

I hope you are presently experiencing your relationship dreams, but there is a chance you are still hoping they will come true. You *can* have a dream relationship while you are awake. It may not manifest overnight, but when you partner with God and surrender your will to His, your relationship dream will come true at His appointed time!

Like money, your love grows and flourishes when it is deposited and actively invested in the right, God-chosen date or mate. At the bank, your deposits into the right checking, savings and money market accounts will earn interest. With those, your return over time is greater than your initial deposit. But some accounts do not earn interest. Investing generously in God's divine relationship will yield high returns of personal fulfillment. Great relationships require frequent deposits of work, energy, creativity and mutual sacrifices to bless your love. Does your return show that you are depositing love in the right or wrong account?

Kingdom Companionship

There is a major difference in a relationship you join together and one that is ordained by God. God wants you to experience *love without the drama* through what I call *kingdom companionship*™. Kingdom companionship is when you are in relationship with the specific person God created especially for you to maximize your enjoyment of life and fulfill His divine will and calling.

Kingdom companions are anointed by God to celebrate and minister to each other and their connection is evident. Their supernatural joy is often misinterpreted by the carnally minded as sexual attraction, but it is much higher than that. It is spiritual magnetism and a distinctly unique flow of love that feels like a heavenly dream. In fact, their bubbling joy is often envied by others who have settled. No weapon formed against a *kingdom companionship* shall prosper, but weapons will be formed. The enemy launches his best darts because *kingdom companions* are a major threat to him. One can chase 1,000, but two can put 10,000 enemies to flight!

Finally, you must understand that a *kingdom companion* is greater than a soul mate. He or she is what I call your *Spirit mate*™, because your spiritual bond with this divine mate will be phenomenal. This powerful pair can do God's will and work in a way no other couple combination can.

Do not assume that all Christian marriages are *kingdom companionships*, because if God did not ordain a marriage, it isn't. If you are married to your *Spirit mate* now, thank God. If you are single, set your heart on marrying your *kingdom companion*, your *Spirit mate*. Why settle for anyone else?

My "Marinated Love" Revelation

I love how God gives me relevant revelations. Watch out because this one is hot! As a child I was very active in positive activities. I became a youth leader in church and the community's 4-H club programs. I did award-winning projects, demonstrations and presentations on the local, regional and state levels. At my first outdoor cooking competition, I prepared a juicy marinated char-grilled T-bone steak. Let me tell you, my steak was so good that it did not need any Heinz 57 or A-1 sauce. I can taste it now!

I also won the county fair's outdoor cooking competition with this recipe that required cooking wine, soy sauce, ginger, dry mustard and a few other ingredients. Plus, the preparation required marinating time. Then I grilled it to perfection and left just a little pink in the middle. When I cut my sizzling steak, its juices flowed all over the plate.

God has prepared and wants you to experience mouth-watering "marinated love" with your God-ordained mate, but some settle for surface love. To prepare tasty meat, you can shake on seasonings or marinate it. Seasonings stay on the surface. If your mind changes, you can *undo* seasonings by rinsing them off. But, you cannot undo marination. Marination saturates meat *on the inside*. Marinade and meat merge to become *one* delectable, inseparable flavor.

Nobody can undo the Lord's marinated love. Ecclesiastes 3:14 says, "Whatever God does it is forever. Nothing can be taken from it and nothing can be added to it." Like my grilled steak, fire perfects marinated love's flavor so that its aroma and taste linger and endure forever. Alright now!

Stop Trying To Fake It Until You Make It!

You can fool some people some of the time, but you can't fool the Lord any time. Many couples make pleasant public appearances while they are grieving inwardly. Some couples in your neighborhood, some you see at the grocery store, at public events and even at church are unhappily wearing theater masks daily. Many feel stuck in miserable, stagnant, unchallenging, boring, dissatisfying and lonely relationships. Their masked misery is not immediately discerned with the naked eye, but spiritual eyes can see beyond their outward performances. Though a couple may wear matching outfits, that does *not* mean that they are a match made by God. Get a pen and write that one down!

The cliché, "Fake it until you make it," does not apply to marriage well. If you fake it, even for years, you still do not necessarily "make it." As Psalms 127:1 says, "Unless the Lord builds the house, they labor *in vain* that build it." You may try to maintain what God did not ordain, but when your "faking it" sedatives wear off, you will still have pain.

God has built some marriages, but Satan and self have also built some. Let's not get this confused. God created the first marriage, but He did not create or ordain every legal marriage we see today. When God is not the author of your marriage, anniversaries will become more miserable instead of becoming more blissful. The longer you stay together, the more that sick feeling from settling for less than God's best for you will linger. You will never be truly happy or have total peace outside the perfect will of God. "Faking it until you make it" can sap the life out of you.

Tell the truth. It is painful to be bound by fear of what others may say or think, yet some fear man's opinion more than God's. Some compromise their own peace and live in daily depression just to impress opinionated "judges" who will never be satisfied, who do not have a heaven or hell to put anyone in, nor do they know your private distress behind closed doors. Many of these condemning, critical persons masterfully camouflage miserable, dysfunctional relationships themselves and hate to see anyone else truly happy. When you reflect on your past, you may realize that the influence of these slithering serpents helped direct you on a path other than God's perfect will for you and led you to suffer more misery. Their improper advice may have initially seemed sound, but as you look back, time usually reveals its truth and their true motives as you watch their character and romantic relationships evolve--or not evolve!

If you have been living a relationship lie, deal with it. When God opens your eyes to truth and exposes the roots of your error, do not let stubbornness, guilt or shame guide you deeper into disobedience and prolong His deliverance. Receive His correction, extract the good from every lesson and move forward into God's perfect will for your life. Don't remain in the bondage of condemnation by man when you have been confirmed by God. Your mistakes do not change God's opinion of you or His will for your life. Like a loving father, He cares enough to discipline you. He will help you overcome setbacks and set you up for greater comebacks. He can transform your trials into triumphs and turn your tests into testimonies. God is an awesome God!

God Wants You To Experience Love Without The Drama!

Love satisfaction impacts every area of your life. In an ideal world, I could give you five key ingredients and a seven step recipe to a perfect relationship, you would carefully follow each step, and whala-the perfect marriage or dating relationship would appear! Unfortunately we do not live in a utopia. What I can tell you is that if you expect a multiplied return on love you must take a brutally honest look in the mirror and begin to improve that person first.

When you love better, you live better. The opposite is also true. Your heart can become exhausted, worn and weary when you knowingly continue to spend time with the wrong people. Your self-esteem may have been damaged by a belittling, bossy boyfriend or girlfriend, wife or husband. Too many people have settled for less than a whole man or woman so long that they do not know or no longer remember what it feels like to have a healthy relationship. Do not let your past weary you any longer.

In Proverbs 31, Solomon warned his son not to give his strength, his best physical and emotional love, to the wrong women. Be careful ladies and gentlemen. Some have settled for Mr. or Ms. Wrong so long that they reject Mr. or Ms. Right. Don't continue exhausting your energy in the wrong relationship. Stop settling. Save your strength, your best love, to invest in the one God predestined for you.

Memories of a dysfunctional past may make you feel your chance of a sizzling, successful future relationship is slim. That is not true at all. A dramatic past makes you the perfect candidate for a phenomenal future with Christ!

Living And Loving Drama Free

My hope is that you will begin to live drama free and no longer settle for any verbally, emotionally, physically, sexually or even financially abusive relationship when you deserve to have a relationship that is sizzling and satisfying in *all* areas--not just in the bedroom. I also hope that you will allow the Lord to heal you from past heartbreak so you no longer feel insecure, inferior or battle low self-esteem.

If you are single at the moment, know that you do not have to settle for the first person who comes along. People have destroyed their lives and delayed their destinies in desperate attempts to find someone to love and share last names. Pray and seek the Lord in every step of dating. When you feel you are ready to marry, you need to be sure you are uniting with your God-ordained mate, because he or she has what you need to stand with you for the rest of your life. God can give you strength to stand solo until He reveals your divine mate. He won't let you miss him or her!

Do not let haters talk you out of pursuing your dream relationship--the once in a lifetime opportunity God created just for you. You do not have to settle for an incompatible person for public show, fear of loneliness or fear of disappointing a controlling parent, friend, relative or authority figure. Their dream date or mate for you may not be God's dream date or mate. You owe yourself more than you owe others, so do not let anybody manipulate and pressure you to remain in bondage of a boring, unfulfilling relationship or commit to a future with a person who is a random selection and not God's divine choice for you.

God sees the big picture, not just the snapshots we are looking at now. Couples can have all the material things--a nice home, car, career, clothing, large bank accounts--and have a huge void in their lives from unmet emotional needs when they are mismatched ribs. God is trying to spare you that pain. Money can't buy love. It is God's gift.

If you are already married, take time to pray together with hopes that your future will be brighter than your past. Remember that you must regularly invest in the success of your relationship. It takes two to make them work, but if the one person you are with now means anything to you, do your part to demonstrate how special he or she is to you. Verbalize your feelings daily. Do not assume your mate is assured of your love since you said *I love you* last week or after you first met. Actions do demonstrate that you love someone, but people need to hear those words and feel the genuineness of your expression in their hearts.

Great marriages are about partnership. You are not to be each other's gods, but you should constantly strive to fulfill your part of your mate's unmet needs. Both of you should contribute to your marriage in some way--whether financially, emotionally, spiritually and/or physically. You don't have to contribute the same amounts, but you must give more than sexual pleasure to have a thriving marriage.

It takes two willing people to make any relationship a success. Since one of those persons is you, I hope that as you read the insight on these pages, you did not just think of suggestions for your significant other, but I pray you examined yourself and made personal improvements, too.

Drama-Free Relationships Require Two Willing Hearts.

A drama-free relationship is not me-centered, but we-centered. Successful love takes two considerate, attentive givers. If you expect a relationship to grow and satisfy you, each partner has a legitimate responsibility to consider and strive to meet each other's needs. There are times you have to focus on and take care of yourself, but too many persons operate in selfishness and rebellion the majority of the time. Think about it. It is really not logical to expect to receive all that is good when you refuse to sacrifice and sow seeds of love into your significant other. Selfishness is drama.

You may think the relationship you are in now is all about you, but be warned. The brightness of the center of attention spotlight can look attractive, but the intensity of its heat can burn you when it shines on you for prolonged periods of time. Thinking love is all about you can hurt!

You and your love likely have differing backgrounds, so patience and forgiveness must abound when you are trying to deal with and understand them. It is not uncommon for couples to have very different expectations. It may take time for one or both of you to adjust and learn to love on a higher level, but you can do it if God called you together.

Many people have not witnessed positive relationship role models. If you were raised in a single parent home, you may not have seen two people working together as a team toward a common goal. (Don't feel so unfortunate. Some parents were married, but dysfunctional.) God will place positive relationship mentors on your life's path to demonstrate His way to properly handle dates and mates.

Because of familiarity with dysfunction, the absence of proper role models, the lack of successful relationship coaching, counseling or training, little or no spiritual knowledge of God's word, purpose and desire for us in marriage and sometimes just being stupid, stubborn and hard-headed, many people have made tragic relationship mistakes. They have dated and married for every other reason except the perfect will of God. They have fallen into patterns of dating, cohabiting with and even marrying verbally, physically, emotionally, sexually and financially abusive partners. Their ripped and ragged poor self-esteem led them to settle when God wanted to give them a relationship that was sizzling.

When you are insecure, battered or bruised, it is easy to allow people to treat you in ways that they should not. Relationships should be mutually beneficial, not one-sided. Show an overflow of love toward your mate, but make sure you are getting it back. One person should not always be the giver while the other always takes. When you know your value, you won't let yourself be treated like less than who you are. You do not have to tolerate abuse any longer.

Build your self esteem on the word of God which stands forever. Increase your confidence by learning who you are in Christ. Everything that God made was good. He has said that you are fearfully and wonderfully made in His own image and likeness. That means He made you like Him, but He made you so unique that He threw away the mold. He could not duplicate such an awesome creation, so you no longer have to compare yourself to others.

The truth can hurt, but it will help you heal. You cannot make another person be more loving to you, even when you do everything you can to show them love. Some people try to deceive, manipulate and control people into doing what they want them to do. Some who have acted this way for years need to know that this behavior is unChristlike. Also, beware of people who try to disguise their feelings of insufficiency with controlling personalities. Acting like they have answers to everything, they exert unhealthy authority over you and lead you the wrong way to trip you up. That is witchcraft and emotional abuse.

Abuse leaves marks on your heart, but God is a healer. Like a hurting, broken-footed animal in excruciating pain, you may be guilty of snarling and lashing out at the very person God sent to love and nurture you back to emotional health and help heal your past relationship wounds. When God brings a genuinely concerned and loving person into your life after you have been hurt, you must be careful not to abuse and hurt him or her, too.

Many people mishandle a gentle love after having had a roughneck. Now that you realize your mistake and God has healed you, thank your God-sent gift for loving you when you were difficult to love. If they are still there, really thank them for not giving up on you, for looking beyond your faults and seeing your needs. That's what Jesus did.

If you were bruised by divorce or other relationship tragedies, were unequally yoked or in a miserable, unbalanced relationship, forgive yourself. God is a healer and He cares for you. There is healing power in love.

The Healing Power Of Love

Great pain has caused a number of persons to give up on love temporarily. I know badly hurt and disappointed people who say they do not want to ever be in love again. Their wounded hearts don't believe they will find true love. It's hard to see the sun when dark clouds surround you, but time heals wounds. Deep down, most who are not yet healed would welcome genuine and healing true love.

If you are now single because of divorce or death of your spouse, your heart may be heavy and in anguish, but love is a healer. Many who have never been married have spent countless years cultivating relationships they hoped would result in lifetime companionship, but did not. Love is a healer. It is so good to know that after exiting an unhealthy relationship or overcoming the emotional distress of grief, there is healing power in divine fellowship with one who loves God and loves you.

Some are unwilling to risk being hurt by the opposite sex again, so they switch sexes. Do not turn to same sex relationships because a heterosexual date or mate hurt or abused you. Homosexuality conflicts with God's original intention for relationships and marriage. Because it is outside of His original created purpose, it disgusts God. God loves sinners, but He hates the sin of homosexuality. Again, give God all your hurt and let Him heal you.

Jesus can heal the root of physical and emotional pain. Let Him restore you with His love and presence. Read the Bible, His love letter to you. Surround yourself with Christ-like men and women. Friend, you can heal and love again.

The Rhythm Of Love

It takes two separate and unique individuals to blend together in a harmonious effort to make any relationship operate smoothly and function effectively. Do not make the mistake of constantly comparing yours to someone else's. Do not let anyone else's bragging cause you to feel you have nothing to treasure about your courtship or marriage. Just like no two people are alike, neither are two relationships. It may take newlyweds a while before they create a unique "rhythm" for their relationship. Learn what works for the two of you and as long as it's godly, work it!

Beware of the temptation to compare your date or mate to someone else's. Wives, do not expect your husband to do what your friend brags about hers doing. They are two totally different men. And whatever you do, please do not verbally compare him to any other man you respect. That is disrespectful and belittling to the king of your castle.

Although some household management methods may differ by marriages, biblically, the male should always walk in his authority and be a provider for his household. It's okay for his wife, his helpmate, to be an entrepreneurial Proverbs 31 woman rather than a stay at home wife, but God did not intend for all the pressure of provision to be on the wife. He is charged by God and held accountable to cover her. Other minor traditional household duties can be shared. For example, some women like to cut grass and some men love cooking. That's okay. If they can work out this reversal of traditional roles, they should go for it! But, do not get caught or tricked into trying to raise an adult.

Love Can't Sizzle When You Are Acting Like Children.

If one or both of you been acting like a child instead of a mature lover, it's time to grow up. Whether you believe you can or not, you *cannot* raise a grown man or woman. Read that again. God expects adult parents to raise children, not try to raise another adult in a relationship. So why do so many ambitious people think they can help an unmotivated man or woman grow up, be responsible and mature? And why are so many women, especially single mothers, allowing rebellious, irresponsible men who refuse to provide more than sexual stimulation live off of them?

I Timothy 5:8 says if a man does not take care of his own house he is worse than an infidel. Ladies, if you have been wondering why your man does not seem to be taking leadership and responsibility, do not make excuses for him. Examine yourself and how you have been treating him, too. You could have unwisely chosen an irresponsible person from the start. It is also possible that he refuses rise up and provide and support you because you have done everything for him. Not requiring a man to be responsible, even if you are willing to carry more than your share of the household load, cripples him into becoming a lazy adult.

Most children are not required to contribute financially to a household. Women can weaken men by doing everything for them and not requiring them to contribute financially. As a result, the women are weighed down, stressed out and exhausted with the whole burden of household expenses. That was not the way God intended it. God gave Adam responsibility to take care of his wife.

It's healthy to check yourself often to make sure that you have not been acting like you are your mate's mother or father. Proverbs 22:6 admonishes us to train children up in the way they should go so that when they are old, they will not depart from it. When you are old enough to know better, you should do better. Raising young children can be quite a challenge, but thinking you can raise or train an irresponsible adult is guaranteed frustration!

If you have not been getting good responses from your spouse lately, it may be because he or she feels you have been treating him or her like a child. Adults despise being talked to and treated like children. Think about your recent comments and demands to your significant other. If you are acting like your love's parent and not his or her lover, you probably feel unfulfilled right now. Stop creating major arguments over minor things, like cleaning up socks. They should pick them up, but don't major in minor things. You should quickly correct the parental nitpicking if you expect to have romance and satisfaction. Don't keep nagging to get him or her to do what you want done. You can get more results treating him or her like an adult.

You cannot retroact time and be your spouse's parent. Remember that he or she is a unique individual that has already been raised. Be patient and understanding since the two of you were raised differently. Offer life-enhancing input and share in decision-making, but know that it's not your job to even think you can raise him or her over again. As his or her lover, be a positive influence. Your delightful duty is to pour on the love, encouragement and praise!

Your wife is not your mama! Your husband is not your daddy! (I'm not talking about in the bedroom!) Spouses are supposed to be equals. So if you have been thinking that you are the smarter, more superior partner, I hate to burst your bubble of arrogance, but POP! You are a team.

Childish partners also blame everyone else for their mistakes. Have you considered that you might be childish? Yes, you. You may not tell it this way, but he or she may not deserve the blame for everything that's not going right. Though you may feel you're the one who has it all together, you have missed the mark. When you point one finger at your mate, three more are pointing back at you. Look in the mirror. You could be the one with child-like conduct.

In Corinthians 13:11, the Apostle Paul commented, "When I was a child I acted as a child, but when I became a man, I put away childish things." Have you put away your child-like behaviors? When you are angry or upset, do you punish your companion with the silent treatment? Do you stomp off to your room when you disagree or can't have your way? Do you throw fits and temper tantrums so you can be the center of attention? Childish, childish, childish! My friend, it is time to mature, repent to God and to the one He sent to love you all the days of your life.

Marriage's purpose is not to try to raise another adult. Respect your God-given mate. Don't look down on him or her. Do positively influence him or her with loving words, actions and attitudes. The challenge is to do it sincerely from the heart, without any ulterior motives. *You* be the first one to give the mature adult love you want to receive.

Avoid Unnecessary Drama.

You must take authority over drama behind the scenes.

Beware of drama from your mama. Most mamas only want the best for their babies. They have been around the block a few times and know deceivers, counterfeits, players and those who won't last for a lifetime when they see them. Heeding to a godly mama's warnings can pay off. But some mamas are selfish, jealous and dysfunctional. A drama-filled mama's interference can cause you to lose true love. So watch what you tell mama about your love life!

Handle your baby mama drama. If you are a parent, choose to respect your current relationship and teach others to respect it, too. A good friend, a single dad, told me that you mostly have baby mama drama when two people are still intimate or one is leading the other on to think he or she wants to be a couple again. Don't dabble. Demand respect from your ex. Respect your new love, too!

Watch out for leeches who suck the life out of you. Leeches are suttle relationship embezzlers. Tiny losses may go unnoticed, but when those small amounts accumulate, you can wake up one day and your account is wiped out! You don't realize they have sapped your strength until you suddenly collapse! So cut off the takers before they kill you.

Be watchful of golddiggers. Golddiggers do not care about the relationship's quality, but the quantity of Ben Franklins or anything else of value they can receive. They are not givers, but takers. So be mindful. If you flash your material possessions to attract attention, be aware that you may not attract quality dates. You may attract golddiggers.

Are You Investing or Spending Your Time In Love?

God Bless The Child That's Got His Own is a classic song by Billie Holiday. One memorable line I love is, "Money, you have lots of friends hanging around your door. But when the money's gone and the spending ends they don't hang around anymore." That has proven to be a true statement for many people. If you live long enough and have a stable job at a known organization, a booming career or great financial or social status, you will realize its truth, too.

Money is not the only valuable commodity. Time has higher value because you do not know how much more of it you have left. If you lose money, you can get more and replace what you lost by working, investing or other means. But you cannot fully replace lost time except God restores your years. Every day is priceless, so are you spending *or* investing time in your present relationship?

Think of it like shopping. *Spending* happens when you impulsively buy items you want that are not necessities. It's nice to be able to spend, but you can get carried away buying items that do not benefit you. When you *spend*, you waste time when your deposits of love and time spent do not bring increase to you. *Investing* occurs when you purchase items to make your future better. Even though some assets you may purchase will depreciate in value, like a car, you do need transportation to help you go to work, build your business and make progress. Investments bring increase. They build your future and get better over time. You can't get time back. So which will you chose to do with your date or mate, *spend* or *invest* your time and good love?

Don't Let Performers Waste Your Time.

I have learned a lot from past friends and relationships. One of the greatest lessons I have learned is that the enemy does not mind you wasting time. He specializes in sending *similar, but not like-minded* people to perform as friends and lovers to help you do it. You spend a lot of time building them up, but they are slowly draining you. Some sneakily make negative, discrediting remarks about those God has connected your destiny to. Their strong, selfish opinions will have you thinking bad things about others that are not even true. Don't let their negative influences mislead you.

Some changes must happen to make room for true love. If your circle of friends is changing, do not get so upset. It may be God working things together for your good. He could be preparing the way for romantic love to flourish!

God knows who loves you for real and who is hanging close because it benefits them. He prunes the vines in our lives so that we can bear more fruit. Thick and healthy-looking *vines* can deceive you. The vines are not edible. It is the fruit of the vine that can be eaten. So sometimes the thick vine has to be decreased so that the fruit, the valuable part, can increase. Accept His friendship changes. Though pruning is painful at first, it will make you more fruitful.

Matthew 13 explains that wheat and tares get tangled up and grow together, but *at harvest time* God separates them. Let me tell you what God told me. Though it hurts first, don't get so upset when some relationships dissolve. Rejoice! It's harvest time. If you're being separated from old associates, you may be on the brink of a love breakthrough!

Are You Entangled In The Wrong Relationship?

Separation of wheat and tare at harvest time is also true for relationships. Some love changes are on the way for some couples. This may not be what you expected, but I am obeying God and writing it anyway. Someone is holding on to the wrong person. In your heart of hearts you know it. He or she is blocking the true blessing God has in store for you. Let Holy Spirit reveal if this applies to you or not.

Some wheat is dating or married to a tare right now. You know it and you have even felt the tare prick you at times. You have tried to protect the tare and make it look like the two of you are both wheat, but the growing season is over. It is now harvest time. God separates and distinguishes the wheat from the tare at harvest time. The separation may not feel good, but it works together for good. All things work together for the good of them who love the Lord, who are the called according to His purpose.

Unfortunately, every relationship story is not going to be a fairy tale. You can feel entangled by a snare when you are a "leftover love." In Genesis 29, Leah was married and miserable. Deception, not true deep love led her to become Jacob's wife. Jacob was passionately in love with Rachel, her sister and his bride of choice. Jacob's love for her was so strong that he cried when he kissed Rachel, then worked for a total of 14 years before he could marry her. Leah's story reinforces that legal marriage cannot make a person who is not *in love* with you, truly love you. Passion for his or her *true, God-ordained rib* will be undeniably evident.

Ignorance Is Drama!

Don't throw yourself into the wrong relationship! As a teen, I heard older generations use the phrase, "His nose is wide open," when speaking of a young man in hot pursuit of a young lady. If you are dating or mating, more than your nose needs to be open! Your eyes need to be open, too, so you can see drama before it gets close to you.

Everyone who desires drama-free love should seek the Lord, wait to hear His wisdom and watch what He shows you about any prospect. He never lies, so don't doubt Him. The only thing drama-filled persons add to your life is emotional stress. When you let God lead you, His ordained date or mate will add and multiply, not subtract and divide from your relationship with the Lord, your peace and joy.

A drama-filled person is like a pig who loves slop. You can soak it, brush its skin until its pink and pretty, tie a red bow around its neck, kiss it on the cheek and talk to it like an indoor pet. You can take it to the heart of city, buy the best pet attire, take it to see *Animal Farm* and show it a new way of life. However, no matter how much you clean that pig up, it will run back to mud the first chance it gets.

Do not ignore the truth of who someone is. You may try, but you cannot persuade everyone to change for the better. Many are afraid to "step out of the boat" and risk change. Some have become so used to dysfunction that they stick with what is familiar. Since God has given all of us a will, you can't force anyone to make the decision you want them to. You should not use deceptive tactics to manipulate or control anyone either. Use your power positively in prayer!

Your Destiny Does Not Have To Repeat Your History.

My friend, you can experience *love without the drama* when you give God the opportunity He has been waiting for--the chance to lead in your love life. Maybe you never thought that God cared about your relationships. Perhaps you did not even think that the Bible was so practical, containing demonstrations and instructions on how to flow in love greater than you have ever experienced before. Maybe you knew that the Bible had wisdom to build relationships, but thought that God's kind of love and marriage was unachievable with dates you have met so far.

Some people used to think God's guidelines were too great. Many rebellious refused to read the Bible's free help. The flesh of some who were single and sexin' stayed away from the Word to avoid God's conviction. Still others, even Christians, were stubborn like Jonah, who refused to totally submit to God and tried to run from His perfect will when he wanted to be in total control. You can never outrun God.

Some persons are suffering right now because they have moved too fast into the wrong relationships. Some did their best to rebound after heartbreak, but fell flat on their faces. A great number walked by fear instead of by faith. They were so afraid of getting hurt that they let fear rule above the faith they did have and ended up settling for less than what God had intended and ordained for them. Others were mishandled, are still hurting and are not yet healed. If this is you, you do not have to let recollections of past relationship mishaps hinder you from experiencing the wonderful future that God has prepared just for you.

Why be stubborn and keep holding on to heartbreak? Drop it like a hot potato and don't hold on to it any longer. Release all bitterness and unforgiveness. If are still hurting from an ex-lover's rejection, grab your healing and rejoice. God did not reject you and never will. Do not repeat your past mistakes and do not be entangled again in any relationship that is a yoke of bondage. God's yoke is easy and His burden is light. It's time to try living and loving God's way. You have absolutely nothing of value to lose!

God did not give one biblical instruction that will hurt you. Just like the serpent did in the garden, the devil will try to twist God's true intentions to make you think that God is holding back or too strict on you. That slick serpent tricked them then and the devil is still a liar today. Adam's and Eve's disobedience resulted in curses that impacted them and future generations. You, too, must be mindful that disobeying God may consequently impact your children, grandchildren and generations after them.

Your relationship destiny does not have to repeat your history. The Bible says that wise men leave an inheritance, not a curse for their children's children. Today you can start to leave a legacy of love for future generations. Plead the blood of Jesus over them. Rebuke every generational curse of broken relationships, harmful love habits and spirits like witchcraft, manipulation, whoredom, adultery, lust, foolishness and abuse. Your children do not have to be divorced or be single parents if you are. Speak God's specific words of life to decree their future relationship success. Get every drop of love that God has promised you!

Do You Really Know What Love Is?

I hope I have inspired you to get in hot pursuit of God's plan for amazing, overflowing and fulfilling relationships. Real love is not as shallow as the *"Do you like me? Check the box yes or no"* note third graders send. Love is not about how much money you can spend to impress someone who could care less about your heart. Neither is love about having any old person around, even one that's not good for you, because you do not want to be lonely. When you take time to learn and love the scriptures, which were written to make your life better when you follow them, you can learn and discover so much more about what true love really is.

Song of Solomon 8:7 says, "Many waters cannot quench love. Neither can the floods drown it." Lust is short-lived, but love does not die or fail. True love is rooted so deep that it outlasts storms. It surpasses trials and even the death of the object of its affection does not cause love to end.

I Peter 4:8 says, "Love covers a multitude of sins." What a goal it is to learn to love an adult with the unconditional love like you have for children. I know you expect more from adults than children, but I want to emphasize the tenderness of the love we have toward them. As babies, your children, nieces or nephews may vomit on your clean outfit. As toddlers they may write in crayon on your freshly painted wall. As teens they may frustrate you if they act like they had no parental training. In all of these challenges, do you dismiss, reject and stop caring for them? No, because your love for them is greater. There is absolutely nothing they can do to make you fall out of love with them. That's how God loves us. It may seem like a tall order, but He wants us to be able to love everyone, some close and some from a distance, with unconditional love.

I hope that like Apostle Paul in Philippians 3:13-14, you are forgetting those things which are behind you, reaching forth unto those things which are ahead and pressing toward God's mark and the prize of fulfilling His high calling on your life. Now that you are ready to love better so you can live better, let me share these biblical characteristics about love, expressed in I Corinthians 13.

Love is greater than your great speaking ability. (verse 1)
Love is greater than your charisma or gifts. (verse 2)
Love is greater than your charitable contributions. (verse 3)
Love is patient, kind and endures long. (verse 4)
Love is never jealous or envious. (verse 4)
Love is never boastful or haughty. (verse 4)
Love is not rude, arrogant or prideful. (verse 5)
Love is not self-centered. (verse 5)
Love is not easily provoked, touchy or resentful. (verse 5)
Love believes the best, not the worst. (verses 5 and 7)
Love forgives and keeps no records of wrong. (verse 5)
Love rejoices when truth, not wrong prevails. (verse 6)
Love bears up under anything that comes. (verse 7)
Love's hope is fadeless in all circumstances. (verse 7)
Love endures everything without weakening. (verse 7)
Love never ends, fails or becomes obsolete. (verse 8)
Love, hope and faith walk hand in hand, but love is the greatest of the three. (verse 13)

The Greatest Love of All

Before you fall head over heels in love with anyone else, make sure you have fallen in love with Jesus Christ. He is the One who teaches all how to truly love. Unlike past lovers, He will never forsake you and leave you alone. He will never reject you. He promises to hold your hand through any storm or tragedy you will ever face. My friend, you are not alone. Jesus is already in love with you!

Beloved, it is my desire that you will have phenomenal relationship success with your honeybun, but did you know that God loves you much more than he or she ever can? You are the apple of God's eye. John 3:16 says, "For God so loved the world, that He gave His only begotten Son, that whosoever believes in Him should not perish, but have everlasting life." God gave His *only* and *all* for Y-O-U.

Only through a committed relationship with Christ can you truly experience *love without the drama*. To have the best of God's blessings in life and love, you must be born again. Today my friend, can be your day of salvation.

Romans 10:9 declares, "That if thou shalt confess with thy mouth the Lord Jesus, and shalt believe in thine heart that God hath raised Jesus from the dead, thou shalt be saved." If you want to be saved, repeat this sinner's prayer.

Heavenly Father, I repent of my sins. I ask you to come into my heart and make it your home. I believe Jesus died on the cross for me and God raised Him from the dead. Please give me new life. Amen.

Now that Christ is front and center in your life, you can journey from drama to a dream. You are now equipped and empowered to experience God's *love without the drama!*

Now On Stage: The Author
LYNETTA JORDAN

"The Motivator" Lynetta Jordan Is:

A Dynamic Minister, Captivating Speaker, Inspirational Author, Anointed Worshipper, Energized Entrepreneur, College Queen and Powerful Relationship Builder.

Lynetta Jordan has refreshed, motivated and inspired youth, adults, singles, couples, students, organizations, professionals and community groups for over 25 years.

The spotlight is on this radiant radio and TV personality. Lynetta achieved a Bachelor's degree in English-News Media and earned a Master's Degree in Communication.

She has served as keynote speaker for singles and marriage seminars, women's, youth and men's conferences, church services, community and corporate events, graduations, higher education conferences and convocations.

Whether preaching, singing, writing or motivational speaking, "The Motivator" Lynetta Jordan performs for an audience of One, Her Savior Lord Jesus Christ. Through *Lynetta Jordan Ministries* she inspires the world one soul at a time with women's conferences, Bible studies and events.

Send Testimonies, Speaking Invitations And Inquiries to:

Lynetta Jordan Ministries
P.O. Box 1791
Elizabeth City, NC 27906
EMAIL: lynetta@lynettajordan.org

ORDER MORE BOOKS @ www.lovewithoutthedrama.com

www.ingramcontent.com/pod-product-compliance
Lightning Source LLC
Chambersburg PA
CBHW060823050426
42453CB00008B/556